Lecture Notes in Computer Science

Edited by G. Goos and J. Hartmanis

402

Tapan P. Bagchi
Vinay K. Chaudhri

Interactive Relational Database Design

A Logic Programming Implementation

Springer-Verlag

Berlin Heidelberg New York London Paris Tokyo Hong Kong

Authors

Tapan P. Bagchi
Industrial and Management Engineering Programme
Indian Institute of Technology
P.O.·IIT, Kanpur 208016, UP, India

Vinay K. Chaudhri
TATA Consultancy Services
Nariman Point
Bombay 400001, MS, India

CR Subject Classification (1987): H.1.0, H.1.2, H.2.1, I.2.3, J.1

ISBN 3-540-51881-9 Springer-Verlag Berlin Heidelberg New York
ISBN 0-387-51881-9 Springer-Verlag New York Berlin Heidelberg

Printing and binding: Druckhaus Beltz, Hemsbach/Bergstr.
2145/3140-543210 – Printed on acid-free paper

PREFACE

Rapid advances in data processing (DP) began about 1960 facilitating storage of data on magnetic records and files. This marked a major breakthrough in handling and organizing large volumes of accounting, sales, production, personnel or technical data, and gave DP a key foothold in the users' domain. However, these initial file-based data repositories had a "batch" orientation. The file-based approach focused primarily on the processing of transactions, providing only limited support to information management queries. No on-line queries were possible; the user could only get certain reports printed.

In the mid 70's the orientation of electronic DP started shifting. Users insisted that cost of data storage and maintenance be reduced by minimizing **duplication** of data, a serious shortcoming of these early databases. Interest also became strong in getting a database to store besides raw facts the **relationships** among real world objects. This would get closer to how humans discern real objects. Rarely are objects found to exist in isolation. They often relate to other objects in a variety of ways and the appropriation of this knowledge is clearly of considerable value. This shift paved the way for research on transforming stored data into **stored information,** to result in a multifold increase in the utility of a database.

Among the methods devised, the landmark work of Codd (1970) on the "relational model" representation of data quickly came to be regarded as a natural and efficient way of organizing information into databases. Codd's approach was conceptually simple yet formally elegant for it exploited the rich body of set theoretic operations to manipulate data. The key achievement of the relational model was that it showed how one could eliminate duplicate data and thus bring efficiency and integrity into storing information. Not surprisingly therefore many "relational" DBMS products soon became commercially available, promising to aid in the building of high capability databases.

A serious limitation nevertheless remains in these DBMS products. These products assume that the user already has available a good "relational structure" or a good **logical design** for his database, a fundamental requirement to gain advantages of the relational model. Getting the right relations for a database, however, is not yet a trivial step for the uninitiated.

The present work is a comprehensive logic programming implementation of the relational design methodology. It employs TURBO Prolog to test and establish computational viability of the relevant algorithms. It also presents the expert system prototype of a user interface, designed especially for builders of computerized databases who may have no formal training in relational (or any) database design.

The core of this interface is an expert dialog that exploits semantic information that a user can often readily provide about the objects of interest. Thus, rather than lean on the user's familiarity with database design formalisms, the approach discussed here engages the user in an emulated interview--as if the user is talking to a database expert. Internally the system combines Entity-Relationship modeling and normalization algorithms to automatically develop a relational structure which would satisfy design constraints up to the fourth or fifth normal form, ready for transcription to a DBMS.

The authors selected Gottlob's algorithm [14] for the projection of functional dependencies, Loizou and Thanish's method [19] to test loss-less joins, Ullman's algorithm [28] to test dependency preservation, Yao's summary of Bernstein's algorithm [30] to develop the third normal form and Ullman's method [28] to produce the Boyce-Codd normal form. ER modeling-type semantics are employed to handle multivalued and project-join dependencies.

This work has made some deliberate departures from a strictly analytical or algorithmic approach to database design. For instance inter-entity dependence is inferred by making a note of the dependence between/among keys of entities rather than by exhaustively checking each of the attributes of these entities.

Similar departures will be found in the great emphasis laid here on user interrogation with appropriate memory aids, examples and context-specific questioning. Integrity and consistency in user input are established later by lossless join and minimal cover check algorithms. These have enabled the present work to establish that major efficiencies can be achieved in the time required to reach the final design when the user's general knowledge of objects and the environment in which the database will be used is folded as needed into the machine-assisted design process. The result is a significantly faster design process, especially when rigorous approaches would employ algorithms that may be NP-complete.

ACKNOWLEDGMENTS

The authors express their gratitude to the faculty of the IME Systems Optimization Laboratory and the Computer Science and Engineering Department, IIT Kanpur who helped with advice and countless sessions of invaluable discussions as this work progressed.

T.V. Prabhakar, R. Sangal and J.L. Batra provided constant inspiration and feedback. Santosh Gupta, Prashant Kumar, Ashok Mittal, S. Sadagopan and Kripa Shanker abundantly gave material and moral support--often by sacrificing their own priorities. The authors are indebted to the M. Tech. IME classes of 1986 and 1987 who acted as subjects in most of the prototyping work.

The authors also thank their gurus, Jim Templeton (University of Toronto), and H.C. Agarwal, M.P. Kapoor, M.M. Oberai, and A.S. Parasnis (IIT Kanpur) whose teaching and guidance made this long journey of research eventually possible.

This work is dedicated to Vinay Chaudhri's family and to S. Anupam Bagchi and Arun P. Bagchi.

CONTENTS

CHAPTER I

INTRODUCTION AND PROBLEM STATEMENT

1.1 DATABASE--A REPOSITORY OF DATA

"Explosive" is the term that now characterizes growth in the
volume and variety of data which interest today's organizations.
In many of these organizations machine-supported repositories of
information are emerging as a natural choice. One expects that
these repositories will be efficient. One also hopes earnestly
that they will be easier to live with than the stacks or cabinets
that now hold paper files. Happily, these expectations are being
rapidly realized. Many successfully designed and highly usable
computerized data repositories now exist, known in today's
terminology as **databases.**

An important additional expectation also exists. A database may
begin its existence as a simple personnel file or record keeping
system. But it quickly assumes a significant purpose and role:
it begins to support **decisions** in the organization.
Consequently, besides providing fast access to stored
information, a modern database is expected to be **sharable** among
several users. It is also expected to assure **integrity**--it
should provide correct information whenever queried. And it
should be **evolvable**--it should be able to expand with the
organization's growth.

These are considerable demands but perhaps not too surprising. Many databases now form the cornerstone for Management Information Systems (MIS), a collection of databases and decision aids that business, institutions and even governments are now developing to enable them to meet their critical needs of survival and growth.

1.2 DATABASE DESIGN

Far from mere computerized analogs of paper files and folders holding facts and figures, a modern database is a **well-disciplined collection** of information. It is expected to reflect considerably more "realism" in its contents. This is what has made the database today a focus of intense theoretical and implementational study. One now has to analyze closely the intended structure and contents of databases--facts about real world objects or entities, their features or attributes, and their relationship to each other. Improperly designed, a database may at best be poorly organized and inefficient. At worst it would lack integrity and thus fail its purpose and the organization using the database. These consequences are now well-recognized [8].

Several different approaches have been put forth in the past two decades to address this key design challenge: how should information about the items of interest be captured or modeled into tables, diagrams, or other devices that the database would employ? The objective is to minimize inefficiency and integrity-related problems when all information of interest is brought together into a single repository.

A **collection** of logically related tables rather than a single table of data presently emerges as the solution. This creates a modular set of tables of data, which becomes the new design for a database: a decomposition of the traditional monolithic "flat file" repository into a collection of its component tables.

But this process of decomposing the original large single flat file into several smaller tables is not purely mechanical. To model the real world one would have to retain (a) the **features** of objects in the real world that interest us, and (b) the **relationships** of these real world objects to each other. These two requirements must then be built into the decomposition process itself.

Regardless of its size, therefore, the design of a database would now involve deciding (a) how many smaller files or tables one should have and (b) what data items are to be stored in each of these files.

This process begins with **system analysis:** finding out the requirements the database must meet and the constraints it must satisfy. This is a fairly demanding yet inescapable step in the database design process.

Perhaps the hardest part of designing a database is to uncover exactly what is needed by its users and what is known about the environment in which the database will be used. The people who are going to use the database may therefore need to be interviewed repeatedly. Assumptions about the stated relationships among the various pieces of data must be queried again and again. This process of **collecting required background information** for building a database is a critical step in system analysis. System analysis frequently consumes more time than the actual building and implementation of the database.

After the required background information has been gathered, the database designer isolates the smallest units of the usable data into "attributes". These attributes are then grouped into "entities", a separate data file being created for each entity. In the past, many errors committed in grouping these attributes led to inconsistency and anomalies in databases.

In his 1970 paper [7] on the relational approach to modeling data and design databases, Codd suggested ways of grouping the data to form **relations**, a name given to "well-disciplined" data-files. Codd was the first to formulate the principles of **normalization** of data. It has since been asserted by experts and practitioners alike that if one follows these principles, one can create a good design for almost all database management tasks.

1.3 PROBLEM STATEMENT

This monograph is concerned with the normalization phase of database design when the different data files and their contents (a list of appropriate data-items for each file) are decided. The present work was motivated by the following factors.

Several good techniques and algorithms that can yield normalization have recently been developed. These algorithms systematically exploit dependencies among the data to be stored. Nevertheless, perhaps due to its rigor, the systematic approach to normalization has not yet become popular with database builders. As a result, many database implementations continue to be flat files, carrying considerable redundancy and anomalies--a major source of inefficiency and potential lack of integrity in databases (see Figure 1.1). Writing about dependencies and then analyzing them using algorithms is not very interesting. The process is tedious when done manually.

Another problem remains. In the past few years many relational database products (software) for both large and small computers have become available [11, 12]. These DBMS (database management system) products provide very substantial support for the manipulation of the database. However, without exception these products assume that the user already has in view a relational structure and the corresponding details about data files, record contents, keys, etc. before he or she sits down at the console to define files, records, etc.

ROAD MILEAGE:

	ATLANTA	BOSTON	CHICAGO	CINCINNATI	DENVER	DETROIT	NEW YORK	LOS ANGELES
ATLANTA	0	1037	674	440	1398	699	841	2182
BOSTON	1037	0	963	840	1949	695	206	2979
CHICAGO	674	963	0	287	996	266	802	2054
CINCINNATI	440	840	287	0	1164	259	674	2179
DENVER	1398	1949	996	1164	0	1253	1771	1059
DETROIT	699	695	266	259	1253	0	637	2311
NEW YORK	841	206	802	674	1771	637	0	2786
LOS ANGELES	2182	2979	2054	2179	1059	2311	2786	0

Figure 1.1:   A Flat File database showing road mileage between selected US cities. Over 56% of the data is redundant!

"Logically designed", this database would contain only 28 entries for the twenty eight possible city-pairs.

A broad survey of published literature and commercial DBMS products suggests that most of these products do not yet provide assistance in arriving at a good relational structure for the database before the user begins with the physical process of building a database. A relational database should have the **true relational structure** and not be a mere transcription of the traditional flat files on a relational DBMS.

Thus, it would appear that having the theoretical devices alone is not enough. In addition to having access to a DBMS, the common database builder/user would need an easy-to-use **design aid** that would determine the design requirements and constraints and perform normalization for him. The uninitiated user would continue to need this assistance to avoid the problems of inconsistency and anomalies (till other easier-to-use data organizing methods are invented).

The present work is an attempt to fill this void. In this work the computational viability of several relational design algorithms is established first. A personal-computer-based system is then developed that implements many of these algorithms in an intelligent (logically programmed) environment. The objective is to enable the personal computer itself to expertly assist a database builder so that he easily obtains a good relational model for his database. The user of this aid would thus require no special knowledge of the theoretical methods of database design to gain the advantages of a relational model.

When invoked, the system described here engages the user in a dialog, inquiring about the data-items the user wishes to store in his database. In the process the system infers "data dependencies", an essential input for database design algorithms. This inferring of data dependencies by direct user interrogation is a key thrust of this work. Transparent to the user, the system then utilizes these inferred dependencies in arriving at the normalized relational structure.

1.4 ORGANIZATION OF THIS MONOGRAPH

Chapter 2 of this monograph summarizes past research in this area. Chapter 3 introduces the relational model of data representation. Chapter 4 reviews the different database design methodologies and briefly outlines the theoretical design principles. Chapter 5 discusses the algorithms available that produce the "third" , "Boyce-Codd" and "fourth normal" forms of data relations. Chapter 6 describes a logic programming implementation of these algorithms and certain highly effective semantic queries using TURBO Prolog. The monograph ends with a list of possible extensions of this work. The Appendices contain the chronicle of a sample database design session that used the expert software developed in this work, and a complete TURBO Prolog listing of the software.

CHAPTER II

LITERATURE SURVEY: THE METHODS AND MODELS

2.1 THE RELATIONAL MODEL OF STORING DATA

The relational model of data was first proposed by E. F. Codd in
his pioneering paper "A Relational Model of Data for Large Shared
Data Banks" [7], published in 1970. Codd showed that a
collection of tables that he termed relations could be used to
model aspects of the real world and store data about objects in
the real world. Since then the relational model of representing
data has been recognized for its simplicity, uniformity, data
independence, integrity and evolvability [13].

2.2 RELATIONAL DATABASE DESIGN METHODOLOGIES

Two basic techniques for developing the relational design for a
database are presently available in the literature. These are

* Normalization, and
* Entity-Relationship (ER) Modeling

The normalization technique has been expertly discussed by
Ullman [28] and by Date [8], while several others have presented
informal outlines of it [15, 16, 17, 22]. Yao [30] and Ceri et
al. [5] have summarized the various normalization algorithms that
are now available, including some of their own modifications.

Yang [29] has discussed a graph-theoretic approach to normalization.

The Entity-Relationship (ER) model was invented by Chen [6]. Some very useful extensions to Chen's work have been proposed by Teory [25]. A very distinct feature of the ER modeling approach is its emphasis on obtaining a **data view** of the entire enterprise. This view indicates the things or entities about which information is to be maintained, the relationships showing how different entities relate to each other (advisor, parent, owner, part of, belonging to, etc.), and attributes that represent characteristics of entities or relations that would be of interest.

Designing real life databases nonetheless teaches a quick lesson. One can't gain by being a purist. To be effective the approach requires some **mixing** of the top down "enterprise modeling" approach and knowledge of where and in which form data will be used in the enterprise.

2.3 AUTOMATION OF DATABASE DESIGN

In recent years considerable effort has been expended on attempts to mechanize the manipulation of design information to assist in the database design process. The goal is to end up with a computer-generated relational model of data. One well-known project is ISDOS (Information Systems Design and Optimization) of the Department of Industrial and Operational Engineering at the University of Michigan. The objective of ISDOS was to reduce the length of time from requirements determination to delivering a fully operational database. Two modules, PSL/PSA (Problem Statement Language/Problem Statement Analyzer), planned as a "front end" of ISDOS, are now commercially available. These modules are to be used in the system analysis phase of database design - in defining the requirements and developing the design specifications.

Spiegler [24] nearly accomplished the ISDOS objective--to encompass the entire information system development life cycle in automated design. His system obtained design requirements through PSL/PSA. The output of his system was a relational schema. However, one may note that Spiegler made no reference to any specific normal form which the schema produced by his approach would satisfy.

DATAID [1], a project financed by the Italian National Research Council, aimed at the development of a computer-aided methodology for database design. DATAID developed a logical designer called EASYMAP, which produces a relational schema based on the operational performance of the database. It requires specification of requirements and constraints in a special data definition language that employs a variation of the Entity-Relationship model.

A Prolog program to produce normalized relations is available in the literature [5]. It does not, however, deal with multivalued dependencies, which are too numerous in the real world to ignore during database design. The same restriction exists for the commercial information modeling tools now available, such as the ER-Designer by Chen & Associates, Inc. [31]. The work [5] further presupposes that the user will himself be able to write all the relevant data dependencies. Prototyping by the present authors with actual database builders suggests that a comprehensive specification of data dependencies is an uninviting chore and unwieldy for those who are uninitiated.

2.4 SCOPE OF THE PRESENT WORK

In this work, multivalued dependencies have been explicitly considered. Also, the methodology implemented here does not require the user to write the data dependencies. The user is not required to provide input in any specific (data definition) language either. Instead a dialog here engages the user to obtain from him information primarily of a **semantic** nature (the user's general knowledge of objects and the environment in which the database will be used). Such information is much easier to provide yet usually sufficient. (The system automatically determines if it needs more information to complete the design process).

As the user is led through the semantic queries the system keeps compiling design constraints and specifications. The effectiveness of this approach is thus independent of how much the user himself knows about database design methods or data modeling formalisms.

In the extensive prototyping of this approach done with various levels of users, the authors observed repeatedly that when questions were posed in interesting and familiar contexts, users provided information that was correct and pertinent, and required only a minimum of "recycles" of the design.

After the compilation of the relevant design constraints the present system employs closure, minimality, lossless join check and normalization algorithms to automatically complete the design process. The result is a logically appropriate split among the entities into relations and relationships, including the specification of keys.

The automation achieved in this work is thus intended to serve as a bridge between an uninitiated database builder's capability and the benefits of the relational design methodology that experts have evolved in the past decade.

CHAPTER III

OVERVIEW OF THE RELATIONAL MODEL

3.1 AN EFFECTIVE DATABASE STRUCTURE

The relational model of data showed that a **collection of tables** that Codd called **relations** could be used to represent and store data about objects in the real world. In this chapter we summarize the key features of this model and the ways in which relations can be used to store data. The following presentation is patterned after Gray [15] and Date [8].

3.2 GENERAL FEATURES OF THE RELATIONAL MODEL

3.2.1 A Relation

Given a collection of data sets D_1, D_2 ... D_N, not necessarily distinct, R is a relation on those N sets if it is a set of ordered N-tuples $<d_1\ d_2\ ...\ d_N>$ such that d_1 belongs to D_1, d_2 belongs to D_2 ... and d_N belongs to D_N. Sets D_1, D_2 ... D_N are the **domains** of R. The value of N is the **degree** of R. A tuple's components d_1, d_2, ... are called **attributes**.

Informally, a relation may be a table whose columns correspond to attributes and rows to tuples. For example, in the relation **PART** (Figure 3.1) the five domains are the sets of values

representing, respectively, part numbers, part names, part weights, part colors and locations in which the parts are stored. Each row corresponds to a tuple. The degree of the relation PART is 5. The individual data items--part number, part name, etc.-- are the attributes.

PART

P#	NAME	COLOR	WEIGHT	CITY
P1	Nut	Red	12	London
P2	Bolt	Green	17	Plymouth
P3	Screw	Blue	17	Reading
P4	Cog	Red	14	London

SUPPLIER:

S#	SNAME	STATUS	CITY
S1	Smith	20	London
S2	Jones	10	Plymouth
S3	Blake	29	Plymouth
S4	Clark	20	London

BEFORE normalizing:

S#	PQ	
S1	P1	290
	P2	200
	P3	100
S2	P1	50
	P1	100
S3	P1	200

AFTER:

S#	P#	QTY
S1	P1	290
S1	P2	200
S1	P3	100
S2	P1	50
S2	P1	100
S3	P1	200

Figure 3.1

3.2.2 Normal Form

In the relational model every value in a relation (i.e. each

attribute value in every tuple or row) should be **atomic** (non-decomposable as far as the system is concerned). A relation satisfying this condition is said to be in the **normal form** or a standard form. In Figure 3.1 the attribute PQ in the relation BEFORE can be decomposed into atomic components P# and QTY as shown in AFTER. Thus the relation BEFORE is not in normal form whereas AFTER is in normal form.

3.2.3 Keys

In the relational model, in each relation there is at least one attribute with values that are unique within the relation. This attribute can be used to identify the different tuples in that relation. For example, in the relation PART, P# is unique for each tuple. The distinct values of P# may be used to distinguish any given tuple from the other tuples in the relation PART. Thus P# is a key for the relation PART.

Not every relation will necessarily have a "single attribute" key. However, every relation will have some combination of attributes that taken together will have the unique identification property. For example, in the relation AFTER, the attribute set (S#, P#) forms a key. Existence of such a combination is guaranteed by the fact that each relation is a set. Since sets do not contain duplicate elements, at worst all the attributes in a relation taken together will have the unique identification property.

3.2.4 Candidate Key, Primary Key, Super Key

t is possible to have more than one potential key in a relation.
'or example, in PART, if the part name is unique then it can also
be a key. Such **potential keys** are called **candidate keys.** One
key out of these candidate keys is taken to be the key for the
relation and is called the **primary key.** The primary key should
be non-redundant. By this it is implied that none of the
attributes in the primary key is superfluous in ensuring the
unique identification property. For example, in the relation
PART, the attribute set (P#, COLOR) cannot be a primary key.
Here P# is sufficient for the unique identification of the
tuples in this relation; COLOR is superfluous. Such a set of
attributes (P#, COLOR) which contains a key is called a **super
key.**

3.2.5 Foreign Key

A domain in a relation R is called a **foreign key** if it is not the
primary key of R but its elements are the elements of the primary
key of another relation S (R and S not necessarily distinct).
'or example, in the relation AFTER, S# is not a key, but it is a
key in the relation SUPPLIER. Thus S# is a foreign key in the
relation AFTER.

3.2.6 Referential Integrity

To be useful and consistent a relational model should have a
tuple in some relation with a matching value of the primary key

for each occurrence of a foreign key in a tuple in another relation. This is the constraint of **referential integrity**. For example, in the relation AFTER, if at some point in time S# takes a value S5, then there must be a tuple in the relation SUPPLIER with a primary key value S5. Effectively this would model a constraint that no supplier can supply a part unless he is listed in the relation SUPPLIER.

3.2.7 RELATIONAL MODEL: A SUMMARY

i) No tuples can be equal: each must have a different value for the primary key attribute(s), which must not contain null values.

ii) All tuples in a relation must have attributes in the same order.

iii) Values of each attribute must come from a fixed domain. Attribute values must be atomic--they cannot themselves have components.

iv) If a relational database is to be consistent, there must be certain extra constraints imposed on it, such as referential integrity.

3.3 INFORMATION RETRIEVAL USING OPERATIONS ON RELATIONS

All data within a relational database is viewed as being held in tables or relations. Each relation is a model of real-world data relationships. At the same time a relation is a simple enough structure that users can readily understand. A DBMS that supports the relational model can perform well-defined operations on these relations to retrieve information. The three most used operations are **selection, projection** and **join**, described below. The result of these operations is also a relation.

3.3.1 Selection

Select is an operation of selecting some full tuples based on some condition. If one starts with the relation PART (Figure 3.1), the result of selecting tuples with the condition WEIGHT=17 will be the tuples shown in Figure 3.2.

P2	BOLT	GREEN	17	Plymouth
P3	SCREW	BLUE	I7	Reading

Figure 3.2 **SELECT** with WEIGHT=17 on the relation PART

Formally, selection can be defined as follows. Let F be a formula consisting of constants, attributes (e.g. WEIGHT) and certain operators (<, >, =, AND, OR, etc.). Then selection $_F(R)$ is a set of tuples t in relation R such that F is satisfied. In the example shown above, the formula that specifies the intended selection is WEIGHT = 17, which consists of an attribute WEIGHT, a constant 17 and an operator =.

3.3.2 Projection

Informally speaking, **projection** is equivalent to "vertical selection". For example, projection of relation PART with respect the attributes P# and NAME is as shown in Figure 3.3.

```
P#    NAME
---   ----
P1    NUT
P2    BOLT
P3    SCREW
P4    COG
```

Figure 3.3 **PROJECTION** OF PART (Figure 3.1) OVER (P#,NAME)

Formally, a projection may be defined as follows. If R is a relation with k attributes, the projection $\pi_{i1,i2,..im}(R)$ (where i_j's are integers between 1 and k) is the set of m-tuples a_1, a_2 , ... a_m, such that there is a k-tuple b_1, b_2,... b_k in R for which $a_j=b_j$ for j=1,2,...m.

In the above example $\pi_{P\#,NAME}(PART)$ will be computed by taking each tuple in PART and forming a "2 tuple" relation from the components P# and NAME.

3.3.3 Natural Join

To produce the natural join of two relations, first a cartesian product of the two relations is obtained. Then only those tuples are kept that agree on the common attributes. For example, the natural join of relation SUPPLIER and AFTER (Figure 3.1) is shown in Figure 3.4.

```
S#    SNAME   STATUS    CITY        P#    QTY
---   -----   -------   -----       --    ---
S1    SMITH   20        LONDON      P1    290
S1    SMITH   20        LONDON      P2    200
S1    SMITH   20        LONDON      P3    100
S2    JONES   10        Plymouth    P1     50
S2    JONES   10        Plymouth    P1    100
S3    BLAKE   29        Plymouth    P1    200
```

Figure 3.4 **NATURAL JOIN** OF SUPPLIER AND AFTER

Formally, the natural join of two relations R and S, written R $\bowtie$ S, may be defined as follows.

If A_1, A_2, ... A_n are all attribute names used for R and S, then R $\bowtie$ S = $\pi_{i1, i2, ...im}$ $\sigma_{R.A1=S.A1 \text{ and } R.A2=S.A2 \text{ ... and } R.AK=S.AK}$ (R$\bowtie$S), where i1, i2, ...im is the list of all components of R$\bowtie$S in order except the components $S.A_1$, ...$S.A_k$.

Various combinations and permutations of selection, projection and natural join are used in practice to retrieve information from a collection of normalized relations in a relational database. Many of these have now been implemented on commercial DBMS in the form of SQL (Structured Query Language) and other specialized devices. The actual data retrieval process thus becomes transparent to the user making the query. The user only sees the output as a relation.

CHAPTER IV

RELATIONAL DATABASE: DESIGN METHODOLOGIES

4.1   DATA AND INFORMATION

The two common techniques for relational database design are

     i)   Normalization, and

     ii) Entity-Relationship Diagrams.

In both of these techniques the starting point is **data oriented
information** generated from system analysis of the environment
where the database is needed.   The outcome of the design process
is a relation schema, that is, a collection of well-disciplined
data files, for the database. This scheme specifies and describes
which files should be created and what their contents should be.
The design principles employed here are stated as normal forms,
which are formal statements about how data items when put in the
database are allowed to depend on each other.   Overall, normal
forms are the most valuable principles now available for
redundancy reduction and the removal of anomalies that may
develop in databases, as shown below.   In this chapter both these
design techniques will be described with the help of examples.

4.2   NORMALIZATION

The normalization approach to relational database design takes
dependencies among the data-items as input. Various design

principles are stated in terms of "normal forms". Normal forms are certain standard structures for files that eliminate several database management problems that may develop in real life.

How the different data-items depend on each other is termed "data dependency". In normalization, dependencies are closely analyzed to produce schemata that would satisfy specific design criteria named as particular normal forms "first", "second", "third", BCNF", etc.

Consider, for example, a database which is intended to be the personnel information system of a nationwide chain of automobile repair shops. The data-items to be stored as identified by the analysis of the needs of this organization are shown below.

MECHANIC NUMBER	(MECH NO)
SKILL NUMBER	(SKLL NO)
SKILL CATEGORY	(SKILL CAT)
MECHANIC NAME	(MECH NAME)
MECHANIC AGE	(MECH AGE)
SHOP NUMBER	(SHOP NO)
SHOP CITY	(CITY)
SHOP SUPERVISOR	(SUPV)
MECHANICS' SKILL	(SKLL)
PROFICIENCY LEVEL	(PROF)

1. MECH NO -->>SKLL NO
2. MECH NO --> MECH NAME
3. MECH NO --> MECH AGE
4. MECH NO --> SHOP NO
5. MECH NO --> SUPV
6. SKLL NO --> SKLL CAT
7. SKLL NO -->> MECH NO
8. SHOP NO --> MECH NO
9. SHOP NO --> SUPV
10. SHOP NO --> CITY
11. MECH NO, SKLL NO --> PROF

Figure 4.1: DATA-ITEMS   Figure 4.2: DATA DEPENDENCIES

It is clear from the data-items listed (see Figure 4.1) that the objective of the personnel database will be to keep track of the company's mechanics, their skills, their locations and various other associated information.

4.2.1 Data Dependencies

Figure 4.2 shows the dependencies among the data-items. The single-headed arrows (-->) indicate unique identification. Thus Dependency Number 2 indicates that for a given Mechanic Number there is only one associated Mechanic Name. Dependency Number 10 indicates that for a given Shop Number, there is exactly one City associated with it. The sample data of Figure 4.3 verifies this; given Mechanic Number = 52, Mechanic Name is uniquely identified as Peter. And given that Shop Number = 44, Bombay is uniquely identified as the corresponding city. The inverse of these dependencies may not necessarily be true. There may be several Peters in the company and several shops in Bombay. This type of data dependency (unique identification of one attribute by another) is known as **functional dependency,** formally defined as follows.

Definition 4.1: Functional Dependency

Let R be a relation scheme with attributes $(A_1, A_2, ..., A_n)$, and let X and Y be subsets of $[A_1, A_2, ..., A_n]$. It can be said that X --> Y (read as X functionally determines Y) if for any pair of tuples r and t in R,

$$r[X] = t[X] \quad \text{implies} \quad r[Y] = t[Y]$$

Alternatively, X --> Y is a **constraint** that requires any two tuples to agree on their Y values whenever they agree on X values.

The double-headed arrows (-->>) in Figure 4.2 indicate **multiple association**. An instance (e.g. MECH NO = 47) of the data-item on the left may be associated with several instances of the data-item on the right (e.g. SKLL NO=113 and 55). Thus Dependency Number 1 says that an employee may have several skills. Similarly, Dependency Number 8 says that a shop may have several mechanics working in it.

4.2.2 Problems in Database Design

Even though satisfactory at first glance, Figure 4.3 is a really poor design for the personnel database. First, note the redundancy. The second and third lines (tuples) in Figure 4.3 repeat the same MECH NAME, MECH AGE, SHOP NO, SHOP CITY & SUPV. But there are worse problems with this design.

Suppose that at some time John is transferred from Bombay to Madras and that the organization should therefore record this change in its personnel information system (Figure 4.3) to keep it current. Then all the tuples corresponding to John (MECH NO = 47) will have to be altered (to make CITY = Madras) resulting in a clear inefficiency and thus extra overhead in the updating process. Further, if some of the tuples containing John are inadvertently left unaltered, the database will become inconsistent.

MECH NO	SKLL NO	SKLL CAT	MECH NAME	MECH AGE	SHOP NO	CITY	SUPV	PRO
92	113	BODY	HARRY	22	52	DELHI	JAY	3
47	113	BODY	JOHN	41	44	BOMBAY	CHRIS	5
47	55	ENGN	JOHN	41	44	BOMBAY	CHRIS	1
43	55	ENGN	ANAND	23	44	BOMBAY	CHRIS	6
52	21	AXLE	PETER	25	21	MADRAS	BOB	2
52	28	TIRE	PETER	25	21	MADRAS	BOB	6

Figure 4.3 A "FIRST PASS" DESIGN (THE PERSONNEL INFORMATION SYSTEM

MECH NO	SKLL NO	SKLL CAT	MECH NAME	MECH AGE	SHOP NO	CITY	SUPV	PR
92	113	BODY	HARRY	22	52	DELHI	JAY	3
47	113,55	BODY,ENGN	JOHN	41	44	BOMBAY	CHRIS	5
43	55	ENGN	ANAND	23	44	BOMBAY	CHRIS	6
52	21,28	AXLE,TIRE	PETER	25	21	MADRAS	BOB	2

Figure 4.4 EXAMPLE OF NON-ATOMIC ATTRIBUTES (SKLL NO and SKLL-CAT)

Also, if Harry is the only mechanic in Shop Number 52 and he
quits, all tuples concerning him will have to be deleted. But at
the same time, the information that Jay is the supervisor of Shop
Number 52 will also become deleted. Thus, if the database is
designed as Figure 4.3, these two fundamentally different pieces
of information (i.e. who are the current employees of the company
and which supervisor looks after which shop) cannot exist in it
separately as they should. A brief deliberation will show that a
similar, but reversed problem might develop in adding data to
this database.

Thus a poor tabular design for a database may cause problems of
redundancy and **addition/update anomalies.** Normal forms evolved
in the relational methodology as an attempt to do away with these
problems.

4.2.3 The First Normal Form

The "first normal form" is the same as Codd's standard normal form [7]. It has the property that every data entry for each attribute is **non-decomposable**. For example, Figure 4.3 is the first normal form representation of Figure 4.4. In Figure 4.3, every attribute entry in each tuple consists of only one piece of non-divisible data (BODY and ENGINE in separate tuples for MECH NO=47). Admittedly, the first normal form representation of data is not, by itself, helpful or sufficient as a redundancy-controlling arrangement. However, it is an important starting point for further work to improve the design of a database.

4.2.4 The Second Normal Form

One may verify that the (MECH NO, SKLL NO) combination of attributes is a valid key for the relation in Figure 4.3. This implies that every "non-key" attribute in the relation is dependent on this key attribute (simply called the key). This may be verified by inspecting the single arrow (functional) dependencies listed in Figure 4.2. Note however that while both parts of this key are necessary to determine PROF, only one or other of the two parts of the key is needed to define each of the other non-key attributes, MECH NAME, MECH AGE, SKLL CAT, etc. This hints at one of the reasons why there is some redundancy in the relation of Figure 4.3. (See the repetition of certain data for MECH NAME, MECH AGE, SKLL CAT, etc. in Figure 4.3.)

Figure 4.5 shows the same data in the **second normal form** (keys shown bold-faced). The original data of Figure 4.3 has been divided now into three relations, each of which has the property that the entire key is required to define each of its non-key attributes. Several attributes are duplicated during the process among the three relations. For instance, MECH NO, which appeared only once as an attribute in first normal form (Figure 4.3) now appears both in the MECHANIC table and the PROFICIENCY table. However, one may verify that the total number of attribute occurrences has reduced, from 54 to 50, indicating a net decrease in data redundancy.

MECHANIC:

MECH NO	MECH NAME	MECH AGE	SHOP NO	CITY	SUPV
92	HARRY	22	52	DELHI	JAY
47	JOHN	41	44	BOMBAY	CHRIS
43	ANAND	23	44	BOMBAY	CHRIS
52	PETER	25	21	MADRAS	BOB

SKILL:

SKLL NO	SKLL CAT
113	BODY
55	ENGN
21	AXLE
28	TIRE

PROFICIENCY:

MECH NO	SKLL NO	PROF
92	113	3
47	113	5
47	55	1
43	55	6
52	21	2
52	28	6

Figure 4.5   PERSONNEL INFORMATION SYSTEM IN THE SECOND NORMAL FORM

Note that the individually identifiable (distinct) areas of knowledge (closely related bits of information) are now represented in three distinct relations rather than one single

repository (although this decomposition has not yet reached the
ultimate required level of decomposition, as will be seen soon).

4.2.5 The Third Normal Form

The SKILL and PROFICIENCY relations in Figure 4.5 are both free
from the redundancy in the non-key attributes. In fact they are
both already in the **third normal form**. However, a glance at the
MECHANIC relation reveals some residual redundancy in non-key
attributes. For example, both Tuple Number 2 and Tuple Number 3
state that Shop Number 44 is in Bombay and is supervised by
Chris. Nonetheless, the relation MECHANIC satisfies the
condition for the second normal form (i.e. full key is required
to determine the non-key attributes).

The problem of (Bombay, Chris) being repeated is caused by the
dependency that exists between SHOP NO and CITY, and between
SHOP NO and SUPV (Dependencies Number 9 and 10 of Figure 4.2).
Note here that while SHOP NO identifies CITY and SUPV, it is
clearly not a valid key for the entire relation "MECHANIC". Thus
the situation here is of one non-key attribute identifying some
other non-key attributes. The situation is another example of
fundamentally different kinds of information being mixed together
in the same relation. This mixing causes the occurrence of
redundancy in the relation MECHANIC of Figure 4.5.

MECHANIC:

MECH NO	MECH NAME	MECH AGE	SHOP NO
92	HARRY	22	52
47	JOHN	41	44
43	ANAND	23	44
52	PETER	25	21

SHOP:

SHOP NO	CITY	SUPV
52	DELHI	JAY
44	BOMBAY	CHRIS
21	MADRAS	BOB

SKILL:

SKLL NO	SKLL CAT
113	BODY
55	ENGN
21	AXLE
28	TIRE

PROFICIENCY:

MECH NO	SKLL NO	PROF
92	113	3
47	113	5
47	55	1
43	55	6
52	21	2
52	28	6

Figure 4.6   PERSONNEL INFORMATION SYSTEM IN THIRD NORMAL FORM

Figure 4.6 represents the data of Figure 4.5 in third normal form. A new relation, SHOP, has been created to separate out the shop-related data. Thus in third normal form it can be said that there does not exist a situation where a non-key attribute identifies another non-key attribute. The definition of third normal form is formally given as follows.

Definition 4.2: Third Normal Form

If whenever a functional dependency X --> A holds for relation R, and A is not in X then either X is a superkey for R or A is an attribute in the key.

Note that if a non-key identifies a key attribute, then it will not be a violation of the third normal form.

4.2.6 Boyce-Codd Normal Form

There are some infrequent cases in real life where the third
normal form condition, that no situation exists where a non-key
attribute identifies another non-key attribute, is found
insufficient to reduce redundancy. One such case is shown in
Figure 4.7.

```
STUDENT    COURSE   TEACHER
-------    ------   -------
Smith      MATH     Stuart        STUDENT, COURSE --> TEACHER
Ellis      MATH     Gupta         TEACHER --> COURSE
Chu        MATH     Gupta
Smith      PHYSICS  Roy
Ellis      PHYSICS  Roy
```

Figure 4.7   KEY ATTRIBUTE DEPENDENT ON NON-KEY ATTRIBUTE

A moment of reflection will show the redundancy being caused by
the dependency (TEACHER --> COURSE), in which a non-key
attribute is determining a key attribute. Thus for a relation to
be in Boyce-Codd normal form, whenever an attribute states a fact
about another attribute, it must be able to act as a key for the
full relation. The definition here may be formalized as follows.

Definition 4.3:   Boyce-Codd   Normal   Form

If whenever X --> A holds in R and A is not in X, then X is a
superkey for R.

4.2.7   The Fourth Normal Form

The fourth normal form deals with **multiple associations** among the attributes. To make the concept of multiple associations clear, let us assume for a moment that (in the context of the personnel information system of Figure 4.1) a shop may have more than one supervisor.

If Shop Number = 21 now has two supervisors, Bob and Katz, it would be necessary to add two additional tuples to the relation in Figure 4.3, corresponding to Bob and Katz respectively. The resultant tuples are shown in Figure 4.8. The fourth normal form deals with such repetitions (redundancy) and requires that there should be not more than one multi-valued fact in the same relation. Figure 4.9 shows the fourth normal form representation of the same data.

A formal definition of fourth normal form may now be given [9]. However, we should first formally state what a multi-valued dependency is.

Definition 4.4: Multivalued Dependency(MVD)

Let R(X,Y,Z) be a relation. Each of X, Y and Z may be an individual attribute or a set of attributes, but they are to be pairwise disjoint. Let x, y, z denote the individual attribute entries in the relation.   Define

$$Y_{xz} = [Y: (x,y,z) \text{ is a tuple in } R].$$

The multivalued dependency $X \longrightarrow\!\!\!> Y$ is said to hold for R(X, Y, Z) if: Y_{xz} depends only on x; that is $Y_{xz} = Y_{xz'}$ such that Y_{xz} and $Y_{xz'}$ are non-empty. For example, consider Figure 4.8, with

X = [MECH NO], Y = [SKLL NO, SKLL CAT, PROF],
and Z = [MECH NAME, MECH AGE, SHOP NO, CITY, SUPV, PROF]

The MVD X -->> Y exists because

$Y_{52,[PETER,25,21,MADRAS,BOB]} = Y_{52,[PETER,25,21,MADRAS,KATZ]}$

MECH NO	SKLL NO	SKLL CAT	MECH NAME	MECH AGE	SHOP NO	CITY	SUPV	PROF
92	113	BODY	HARRY	22	52	DELHI	JAY	3
47	113	BODY	JOHN	41	44	BOMBAY	CHRIS	5
47	55	ENGN	JOHN	41	44	BOMBAY	CHRIS	1
43	55	ENGN	ANAND	23	44	BOMBAY	CHRIS	6
52	21	AXLE	PETER	25	21	MADRAS	BOB	2
52	28	TIRE	PETER	25	21	MADRAS	BOB	6
52	21	AXLE	PETER	25	21	MADRAS	KATZ	2
52	28	TIRE	PETER	25	21	MADRAS	KATZ	6

Figure 4.8: EXAMPLE OF A "MULTIVALUED" DEPENDENCY (SHOP NO -->> SUPV)

MECHANIC:

MECH NO	MECH NAME	MECH AGE	SHOP NO
92	HARRY	22	52
47	JOHN	41	44
43	ANAND	23	44
52	PETER	25	21

SKILL:

SKLL NO	SKLL CAT
113	BODY
55	ENGN
21	AXLE
28	TIRE

SHOP LOCATION:

SHOP NO	CITY
52	DELHI
44	CHRIS
21	MADRAS

PROFICIENCY:

MECH NO	SKLL NO	PROF
92	113	3
47	113	5
47	55	1
43	55	6
52	21	2
52	28	6

SUPERVISOR:

SHOP NO	SUPV
52	JAY
44	CHRIS
21	BOB
21	KATZ

Figure 4.9: THE PERSONNEL INFORMATION SYSTEM IN FOURTH NORMAL FORM

The definition of the multivalued dependency may be modified to obtain a definition for functional dependency by requiring that Y_{xz} depends only on x as well as Y_{xz} is a set containing at most one member. Thus functional dependency is a special case of multivalued dependency.

The multivalued dependencies X -->> [] (the empty set of attributes) and X -->> Y in the relation R(X,Y) necessarily hold. They are, therefore, known as the trivial MVDs.

Definition 4.5: Fourth Normal Form

A relation R is in the fourth normal if whenever a non-trivial multivalued dependency holds for R, then so does the functional dependency X --> A for every attribute A in Y.

4.2.8 Higher Normal Forms

As the relational database design theory evolved, new problems were discovered and solutions emerged. One problem that has been specifically identified involves fourth normal form data that still contains some redundancy. The solution has been termed as the fifth or project-join normal form [10]. It appears though that this problem is not "pathologically rare" as it was once thought to be. Here the attributes involve what is termed as a **join dependency** (JD).

To illustrate a JD let us begin with a relation that has two MVDs. Assume that certain technicians represent certain companies and also specialize in servicing certain models of

computer.   The following relation, BUSINESS, embodies these two
constraints.

BUSINESS:

Technician	Company	Model
Smith J	IBM	PS2
Smith J	IBM	AT
Smith J	IBM	RT
Smith J	Compaq	PC+
Smith J	Compaq	AT
Smith J	Compaq	Portable
Smith J	DEC	RT
Smith J	DEC	Rainbow
Chow D	Compaq	PC+
Chow D	Compaq	AT
Chow D	Compaq	Portable
Chow D	DEC	RT
Chow D	DEC	Rainbow
Chow D	IBM	PS2
Chow D	IBM	AT
Chow D	IBM	RT

An application of Definition 4.4 will show that the above relation
contains two MVDs, namely

   Technician -->> Company   and   Company -->> Model.

It is clear that the relation BUSINESS contains some redundancy
due to these MVDs and may be reduced to the fourth normal form by
decomposing into two relations

REPRESENTS:

Technician	Company
Smith J	IBM
Smith J	Compaq
Smith J	AT&T
Smith J	DEC
Chow D	Compaq
Chow D	DEC
Chow D	IBM

SELLS:

Company	Model
IBM	PS2
IBM	AT
IBM	RT
Compaq	PC+
Compaq	AT
Compaq	PORTABLE
DEC	RT
DEC	Rainbow

One may verify that REPRESENTS and SELLS when joined together reproduce the original relation BUSINESS.

Let us now assume that an additional constraint exists in this enterprise. Not all technicians are trained to service all computer models. Thus if Chow D can only service the Portable and Rainbow models, it would not be correct to show him capable of servicing the models PC+, RT, AT and PS2 as shown in BUSINESS. Thus the relation BUSINESS can no longer function as our database.

Similar constraints may also exist for Smith J . It may turn out that he has trained to repair the AT, RT and PS2 models only. Again the relation BUSINESS does not correctly represent these constraints.

The solution would be if one somehow also incorporated the constraint

        Technician -->> Model

into the database. This can be achieved if we join BUSINESS with the relation TRAINING as follows.

TRAINING:

Technician	Model
Chow D	Portable
Chow D	Rainbow
Smith J	AT
Smith J	RT
Smith J	PS2

The join of relations BUSINESS and TRAINING then reflects possible valid combinations of the attributes Technician, Company and Model that coexist in the database, reflecting a set of facts and not fiction. This is shown below in the relation SERVICEMEN.

SERVICEMEN

Technician	Company	Model
Smith J	IBM	PS2
Smith J	IBM	AT
Smith J	IBM	RT
Smith J	Compaq	AT
Smith J	DEC	RT
Smith J	DEC	Rainbow
Chow D	Compaq	Portable
Chow D	DEC	Rainbow

Any relation containing a JD (such as the relation SERVICEMEN above) would be at least a three-way join of three sets of attributes that have MVDs between any two attribute sets taken as a pair.

A relation containing a JD (such as SERVICEMEN) will contain redundancy. To remove these one must decompose the relation to the fifth normal form, i.e. into component relations (REPRESENTS, SELLS and TRAINING in above) that when joined reproduce the original relation.

4.2.9 Value of Normalization

Normalization guidelines reduce redundancy in a database but are biased toward the assumption that the non-key attributes in the database will be updated (i.e. changed) frequently.

Normalization guidelines tend also to penalize retrieval, since data which may have been retrievable from one tuple in an unnormalized design may have to be retrieved from several tuples in the normalized design. However, in general, normal forms provide the most valuable principles now available for redundancy reduction and the removal of anomalies.

4.3 THE ENTITY RELATIONSHIP MODEL

Invented by Chen [6], the Entity-Relationship (ER) approach to modeling (or representing) data adopts what by comparison is a more natural view of data. Some extensions to Chen's work have been made by Teory [25].

The ER model assert that the real world consists of **entities** and **relationships.** Entities are the objects around us about which data is collected and stored. Relationships acknowledge that these objects are somehow connected or related to one another, e.g. a child has a parent, or a particular automobile has an owner. Representation of information using the ER model thus incorporates some of the semantics of the real world. The ER model can be specialized to set theoretic representation and the relational approach to model real life data.

The process of evolving a relational database design using the ER model is summarized in Figure 4.10. Real world "primitives" (data items) are first represented by conceptual primitives (in ER modeling terminology). After the information structure has been completely identified, usually in the form of a diagram

(Figure 4.12), the ER model is transformed into a collection of normalized relations.

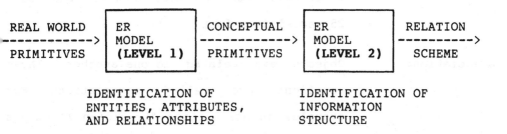

Figure 4.10

4.3.1 Primitives in Real world

Objects: These are phenomena that can be represented by nouns. A person, a place, a thing, an event or an instruction--all are "objects".

Object Class: Certain objects are lumped together into classes based on similarities, e.g. PEOPLE is an object class.

Properties: Objects have properties. A property is a characteristic of an object. For instance, AGE is a property of a MECHANIC.

Property Value set: This is a collection of all possible instances that a particular property may have, e.g. the list of all the skills which a mechanic may have.

Fact: A fact is an assertion that, for a given object, a particular property has a particular element (value) from the Property Value Set. For instance, "AGE of Peter is 25 years" is a fact.

Association: Objects are **related** to one another. These relations are called associations. For example, an association "Proficiency" exists between objects Mechanic and Skill.

4.3.2 Primitives in the Conceptual World (Level 1)

Reality is modeled by adopting a **representation** of it. For example, if one intends to store "IIT Kanpur" in a database, the database will store a representation of IIT Kanpur and not the institution IIT Kanpur itself. Thus, there corresponds a **conceptual primitive** for each of the real world primitives of Section 4.3.1. This correspondence is indicated below.

Real World Primitives	Conceptual Primitives (Representation in ER model)
Object	Entity
Object Class	Entity Class
Property	Attribute
Property Value Set	Domain
Fact	Value
Association	Relation

The Entities, Attributes and Relationships so identified can be displayed using ER diagrams. A **rectangular box** is used to represent **entity types**, the **diamond shaped box** represents a **relationship** between entities and a **oval** figure represents the **attributes.** Figure 4.11 lists the rules employed to distinguish between Entities and Attributes.

Rules for Identifying Entities

1. Entities have descriptive information, identifying attributes do not.

2. Multivalued attributes should be classified as entities.

3. Attach attributes to those entities that the attributes describe most directly.

4. Avoid composite identifiers.

Figure 4.11

Figure 4.12 (see next page) is an Entity-Relationship Diagram for the attributes and relationships shown in Figure 4.6. SHOP, MECHANIC and SKILL have been identified as three entities. Relationships between SHOP and MECHANIC and between MECHANIC and SKILL are appropriately displayed.

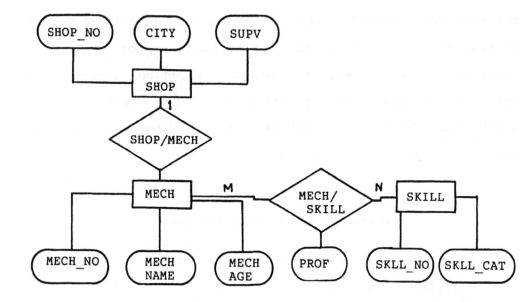

FIGURE 4.12: ENTITY RELATIONSHIP DIAGRAM FOR THE
PERSONNEL INFORMATION SYSTEM OF FIGURE 4.6

4.3.3 ER MODEL (Level 2):   The Information Structure

The entities, relationships and attributes identified at Level 1
are still conceptual objects.   Level 2 deals with the
representation of entities and relationships that uses a set of
transformation rules, summarized below from Chen's work [6].

i)   The set of attributes of each entity in the ER diagram
    becomes a **elation** or file, with the unique identifying
    attribute in this set becoming the key.

ii) The identifying attribute of the entity on the "one" side in
    a **one-to-many** relationship must be duplicated and made one
    of the attributes of the relation, based on the entity on
    the "many" side of that relationship.

iii) If there is a **multilevel hierarchy** of entities, then such duplication must be propagated throughout the hierarchy when converting it to relations.

iv) Relations must be created from the many-to-many relationships. The key for such a relation will consist of the identifying or key attributes of the two entities involved. The non-key attributes will be the relationship modifiers (the attributes attached to the diamond-shaped box).

These rules are helpful in real life database design. For instance, consider the conversion of the ER diagram in Figure 4.12 back to the third normal form of Figure 4.6. Notice that SHOP, MECHANIC, and SKILL entities each form the basis for a relation. The MECHANIC relation must contain a copy of the key (SHOP NO) of the SHOP relation because SHOP was the target in the one-to-many relationship in Figure 4.12. The PROFICIENCY relation in Figure 4.6 is derived from the many-to-many relationship between Mechanic and Skill. Note that the key (MECH NO, SKLL NO) is formed from the identifying attributes of mechanic and skill entities, and lastly the non-key attribute PROFICIENCY acts as a relationship modifier.

4.4 NORMALIZATION vs. ER MODELS

Database design using ER models begins with a list of entity types involved and the relationships of interest that exist among them. The philosophy of assuming that the designer knows the entity types at the outset is, nevertheless, significantly different from the philosophy behind the normalization approach. Both methods assume that a thorough system analysis has been done of the environment where database is needed. However, the ER model approach asserts that one of the outcomes of such analysis is a clear understanding of what distinct entities exist in the environment of concern. The normalization-based approach takes the view that system analysis produces a list of attributes and the relationships among them, and that it is then the responsibility of the normalization process to separate attributes which identify entities (keys) from those which merely describe entities (the non-key attributes). From the implementation standpoint this present work has adopted a flexible attitude, exploiting the strengths of both the approaches, each when appropriate.

4.5 EXTENDED DATA MODELS

Extended data models (a recent innovation) such as the **RM/T** model of Codd [32] have attempted to reflect more of the data structure, i.e. more semantics of the real world. The extended approach involves certain useful and distinct concepts such as entity (any distinguishable object), property, association, etc. Entities are said to possess properties and are linked together by associations. The approach then employs formal symbolic constructs to represent these concepts.

The RM/T model uses **E-relations** for entities, **P-relations** for properties and a **rule** that captures the fact that every property must be a property of some entity: every entry in a P-relation must have a corresponding entry in an E-relation. To collect all properties for a given entity together (an example of manipulating the constructs) the extended modeling approach further provides a set of **operators**. One example is the repeated outer natural join of the RM/T model. The constructs, rules, and operators together constitute the extended data model.

How are the extended models more useful than, for instance, the basic relational model? It is the enhanced richness in capturing reality that gives these models the edge. This point may best be seen in the following table extracted from Date [32].

RM/T Concept	Definition	Examples
ENTITY	A distinguishable object; can be categorized into types	Person, Employer, Department, Supplier, Part, Shipment
PROPERTY	Information that describes an entity	Supplier number, Name, Height, Shipment Quantity, Employer, Department
ASSOCIATION	A relationship connecting entities	Shipment, (Sample-part), Assignment (employee-dept.)
SUBTYPE	Entity type X is Subtype of entity Y if and only if every X is necessarily also a Y.	Employee is a subtype of Person. Engineer is a subtype of Professional

Note that besides ENTITY and PROPERTY, one has here explicit acknowledgment of ASSOCIATION and SUBTYPE.   Note also that the constructs in extended data models, such as the RM/T, are of primary interest to the database designer rather than the user: the constructs expand the designer's capability in conceptually modeling more of the real-world semantics.

Enhanced models have endeavored to expand the database designer's ability to acknowledge the presence of interesting data when he is looking at the real world.   Enhanced models are thus not mere academic extensions.   The present authors have used some of these ideas in designing the dialog (Chapter VI) that appropriately queries the user.   This enables the user to specify aspects of the reality in which the database is to be used somewhat more naturally and without feeling intimidated by formalisms.   As a result, some major shortcuts are made on the way to the final design compared with the path taken in a strictly algorithmic design process.

CHAPTER V

THE DEVELOPMENT OF NORMAL FORMS

5.1 CHAPTER OVERVIEW

This chapter first reviews certain necessary basic concepts, such as closures and projection of functional dependencies. Then it introduces the desirable properties of the decomposed relation schema obtained after normalization. The chapter closes with the algorithms for the third and Boyce-Codd normal form and some comments on the semantics of the fourth and fifth normal forms.

TURBO Prolog implementation of these algorithms is discussed in Chapter VI. The actual program codes are given in Appendix C.

5.2 CLOSURE OF A SET OF ATTRIBUTES

The closure of a set of attributes X, written X^+, with respect to F, a set of functional dependencies (Section 4.2.1), is the set of attributes which can be functionally determined using F, assuming that X is known. For example, closure of the attribute MECH NO with respect to the FD's given in Figure 3.2 is

$$[\text{MECH NO}]^+ = [\text{MECH NO, MECH NAME, MECH AGE, SHOP NO, SUPV}]$$

An algorithm to compute the closure of a set of attributes with respect to a set of FD's was given by Bernstein [4]. In the present work, a version of this algorithm as given by Ullman [28] has been used.

5.3 CLOSURE OF A SET OF FUNCTIONAL DEPENDENCIES

Closure of a set of FD's, written F^+, is the set of all those FD's which can be logically inferred from F.

5.4 MINIMAL SET OF FUNCTIONAL DEPENDENCIES

Ullman [28] has defined the following properties for a set of FD's to be minimal with respect to attribute set Z:

i)   Every right side of a dependency in F is a single attribute.

ii) For every FD(X --> A) in F, there does not exist a set G = F - [X --> A] which is equivalent to F (two sets of FD's, F and G are equivalent if $F^+=G^+$). This means that no FD is redundant in the set F.

iii) For no FD(X --> A) and no proper subset of X is

F - [X -->A] U [Z --> A]

equivalent to F. This means that no attribute on the left hand side of any FD is redundant.

Property (i) is easily achieved in practice, for all FD's may be written with the right hand side as a singleton. To perform the next step (property (ii)), each FD (X --> Y) is dropped in turn from the set F and the closure of the left hand side, X^+, is computed with respect to the reduced set. If the right hand side, Y, is a subset of the closure of the left hand side, X^+, then the dropped FD would be redundant. If Y is not a subset of X^+, the dropped FD is included in the set F. Similarly, to perform the next step to attain property (iii) each attribute in the left hand side is dropped one by one and the closure of the reduced left hand side is calculated. If the closure contains all the attributes on the right hand side, the dropped attribute is deemed redundant and is dropped. If the closure of the reduced left hand side does not contain all the attributes on right hand side, the dropped attribute is not redundant and is kept in the left hand side.

5.5 PROJECTION OF A SET OF FUNCTIONAL DEPENDENCIES

The projection of a set of FD's F, with respect to a set of attributes Z, denoted by $c_Z(F)$, is defined as the set of dependencies $X \longrightarrow Y$ in F^+ such that XY is a subset of Z. An algorithm to compute $c_Z(F)$ was developed by Gottlob [14] and has been discussed by Ceri [5]. It builds a cover for the dependencies holding for Z by initially copying for Z all the FD's in the set F. It then progressively eliminates from them attributes not contained in Z. In the present work the same algorithm has been adopted.

5.6 Desirable Properties of Decomposed Relations

It is generally desired that a relational schema for a databases have the following properties (reasons will be explained shortly):

    i) Loss-less join property

   ii) Dependency preservation property

  iii) Minimality content preserving

Accordingly the design process should test to see whether these properties are being maintained. We begin with a description of each of these properties.

5.6.1 Loss-less Join Property

The decomposition of a relation R into several relations R_1, R_2 by equi-joining the relation R_i over the common attributes. This will ensure that no information is lost in breaking R.

In the past, tableau-based techniques have been used for testing the loss-less join property [28]. In this work an approach developed by Loizou and Thanish [19] has been adopted. According to this approach, for a decomposition to be loss-less, it is necessary and sufficient that the closure of one of the decomposed relations be equal to the original set of attributes. This is very easily verified by checking whether the key for all the attributes is a subset of any of the relations (it may be recalled that closure of the key of a set of attributes is equal to set consisting of all attributes). If this is not so, a relation which has **all** the attributes in the key of the whole set of the attributes is added to the decomposition to ensure loss-less join.

5.6.2 Dependency Preservation Property

The decomposed set of relations should satisfy the original set of dependencies or integrity constraints. If this is not so, the tuples in some of the relations can take values which violate the integrity constraints.

Formally, a decomposition of relation R into $(R_1, R_2 \ldots R_k)$, preserves a set of dependencies F if the union of all the dependencies in $c_{Ri}(F)$ for i=1, 2, ... k logically implies all the dependencies in F, where c_{Ri} is the projection of F with respect to R_i.

An algorithm to test whether a dependency is preserved by a decomposition is given in Ullman [28]. The same algorithm has been used in this work.

5.6.3 Minimality Content Preserving

Decomposition sometimes produces relations in which one relation is a subset of other relations. Such relations are redundant and hence should be eliminated.

5.7 AN ALGORITHM TO PRODUCE THE THIRD NORMAL FORM

The most widely used algorithm to obtain the third normal form from a given set of functional dependencies was given by Bernstein [4]. In this work a version of this algorithm as summarized by Yao [30] has been used. The algorithm gives dependency preserving decomposition. Loss-less join is ensured by the method explained in Section 5.6.1 above. Minimality content is very easily ensured by checking for each relation whether it is a subset of any other relation. The algorithm goes as shown on the next page.

BERNSTEIN'S ALGORITHM

INPUT: A set of functional dependencies H.

OUTPUT: A relation schema P (i.e. set of all the relations) in NF

STEP 1:   (Find Cover)

Find a minimal cover G of H. Also, save G in H'

STEP 2:   (Partition)

Partition G into groups such that all FDs with same left hand side are in one group.

STEP 3:   (Merge equivalent-keys)

i)   J = m (m denotes a null set)

ii) For each pair G_i and G_j with left sides X and Y respectively, do:

[

If X --> Y and Y --> X are in G^+, then

J = J U [X --> Y, Y --> X]

G_i = G_i U [X --> A ¶ A is a subset of Y]

G_j = G_j U [X --> B ¶ B is a subset of X]

Merge G_i and G_j

]

STEP 4:   (Find cover again)

Find a smallest subset G' of G such that

$$(G' \cup J)^+ = (G \cup J)^+$$

Return each FD in J to appropriate group of G' according to its left hand side.

STEP 5:   (Construct Relation Schema)

i)   Let Relation Schema P = m

ii) For each group G_i' do:

$$[$$

$$P = P \cup [X_i]$$

where X_i is set of all the attributes appearing in G_i

$$]$$

STEP 6: Output P

5.8 AN ALGORITHM TO PRODUCE BOYCE-CODD NORMAL FORM

The third normal form relations as shown in Section 5.7 above are first checked to see whether they violate the Boyce-Codd Normal Form. If they do, they are further processed to obtain the BCNF.

To check whether a relation violates BCNF, first the original set of FD's is projected with respect to the attributes in that relation. Then every FD in the projection is taken one by one and a closure of its left hand side is found. If the closure contains all the attributes of that relation (condition for the left hand side of this FD to contain a key), the FD does not violate BCNF and no further processing is necessary. In case a violation of BCNF is detected, this relation is processed by an algorithm given in Ullman [28] to give BCNF. This algorithm is reproduced below.

ALGORITHM TO PRODUCE BCNF

INPUT: A relation schema S and a set of FD's holding for it

OUTPUT: A relation schema in BCNF

STEP 1: Project the given set of FD's over the set of attributes. Find a minimal cover for these FD's.

STEP 2: If there is an FD(X --> Y) in the minimal cover that violates the BCNF, replace S by S_1 and S_2, where S_1 consists of A and the attributes X and S_2 consists of all the attributes of S except A.

STEP 3: Apply this algorithm to the decomposed relations S_1 and S_2 (As S_1 and S_2 have fewer attributes than S, and any relation schema with two or fewer attributes must be in BCNF, eventually a point will be reached where each scheme is in BCNF).

The algorithm ensures a loss-less join decomposition. But this decomposition may not preserve dependencies, hence one may choose instead to apply Bernstein's algorithm to yield the third normal form and then go on to a (weak) fourth normal form.

5.9 OBTAINING FOURTH NORMAL FORM

An algorithm to produce the fourth normal form is given by Lien [18]. However, this is not efficient for implementation because for Lien's algorithm, unlike for instance Bernstein's algorithm, running time increases exponentially with the size of the problem. In the present work the fourth normal form is developed (as in ER modeling) from semantic information on multidependencies solicited from the user. Classifying each multivalued attribute (along with the attributes dependent on it) as a separate entity ensures that there will be at most one multivalued fact per relation. Satisfactory in most practical database design tasks, this approach ultimately gives relations that are in the fourth normal form.

An alternative approach to discover multivalued dependencies would be to reach up to the third NF or the BCNF and then apply the necessary conditions for the existence of MVDs found by Jajodia [33].

Jajodia provides the necessary conditions for the existence of "pure" MVDs (non-trivial and not an MVD counterpart of an FD). He shows that if relation ABC is in the third NF and if A -->> B ¶ C is a pure MVD, then every attribute that is not a member of some key for ABC is an element of A. Further if ABC is in BCNF and A -->> B ¶ C is a pure MVD in ABC then if Ki is any key for ABC then BC is in Ki. Jajodia also shows that if K1, K2, K3 ... Kn denote the keys of the relation schema ABC which is in BCNF then the schema has no pure MVD provided Ki is either empty or is a single attribute.

The last assertion is illustrated by Jajodia as follows. If relation schema R (C, T, H, Rm, S, G) has the FDs (C --> T), (H Rm --> C), (H T --> Rm), (C S --> G) and (H S --> Rm) then one BCNF decomposition of R may be given by

        C S G,   key = C S
        C T,   key = C
        C H Rm,   keys = C H and H Rm
        C H S,   key = S H.

Here relations C T and C H Rm cannot have pure MVD. The only possible MVD in relation C S G is G -->> C ¶ S. And the only possible pure MVD in relation C H S is C -->> H ¶ S. Whether these MVDs actually are there may be verified by checking back the implied semantics with the user or by examining the instances.

The above necessary conditions shrink considerably the database designer's search space for the possible occurrence of MVDs and also join dependencies (JDs).

JDs were introduced in Section 4.2.8. A JD can exist among attribute sets A, B and C only if pure MVDs exist among each of the attribute set pairs AB, BC and AC. Smith [34] shows that if as the logical consequence of pure MVDs A -->> B, B -->> C and A -->> C we can correctly determine all valid combinations of the instances of A, B and C present in the relation ABC then ABC has join dependency; the relation ABC should then be three-decomposed to yield a fifth normal form.

In the (C, T, H, Rm, S, G) example above the only relations that may have JDs are C S G and C H S. However on checking further for MVDs one finds that C S G cannot contain pure MVDs C -->> S ¶ G and S -->> G ¶ C for G is not in the key CS of C S G. This also implies that C S G cannot have a JD and there is no need here to look for JDs any further. Similarly relation C H S also cannot have a JD.

By contrast, the relation S(alesman) C(ompany) M(odel) or S C M with SCM as its key is very likely to have a JD when the following MVDs are asserted:

    S -->> C ¶ M (a salesman may represent many companies),

    C -->> M ¶ S (a company makes several models), and

    S -->> M ¶ C (a salesman sells several models).

A JD may be present among only those relation pairs in 4NF that have composite keys and common attributes in keys. This thus reduces the search space substantially. One may at this point use a "chase type" procedure given by Ullman [28] to infer JDs. Alternatively one may directly exploit the user's knowledge of the environment (semantic constraints). When done with care (as in system analysis), the latter can consistently produce the answer. The questioning is to be done along the following lines.

First isolate the attribute sets where pure MVDs may exist (using the necessary conditions for the existence of pure MVDs as given above). Confirm with the user that these pure MVDs indeed exist. Next, query the user to identify JDs, for instance, by asking

> "You say that a salesman may represent several companies, a company makes several models and a salesman normally sells several models. Is it also true that a salesman sells every model that is made by the company he represents?"

If the user replies "Yes", there in no JD in the S C M relation. If he says "No", a JD exists and S C M should be three-decomposed into SC, CM and SM to yield the fifth NF.

5.10 FINDING THE KEYS OF DECOMPOSED RELATIONS

Lucchesi and Osborne [20] have given two algorithms for finding one key of a relation given its schema and the set of functional dependencies holding for it, and for finding all the keys of a relation given at least one key. In the present work these two algorithms have been used for finding the keys of decomposed relations.

This last step thus fully automates the logical design process for a database.

5.11 CHAPTER SUMMARY

This chapter encapsulates several algorithms and other approaches that have appeared in the literature over the past decade and selects those for Prolog implementation that yield quick results. In particular we select Gottlob's algorithm [14] for the projection of FD's, Loizou and Thanish's method [19] to test loss-less joins, Ullman's algorithm [28] to test dependency preservation, Yao's summary of Bernstein's algorithm [30] to produce the third normal form, Ullman's method [28] to produce BCNF and finally the ER model semantics to handle multivalued dependencies.

CHAPTER VI

PROLOG IMPLEMENTATION OF NORMALIZATION OF RELATIONS

6.1 CHAPTER OVERVIEW

This chapter will discuss the TURBO Prolog implementation of normalization algorithms. This implementation is a key contribution of this work. Unless the reader is familiar with TURBO Prolog, he is advised to first read an introductory text on TURBO Prolog [26]. Appendix A contains a chronicle of a typical database design session with the system developed in this work. The session is illustrated with about thirty interconnected user interface screens. In the text to follow frequent reference will be made to these sample screens. This Chapter begins by giving the overall architecture of the system. Then it discusses the use of TURBO Prolog and design of the interactive user interface. The chapter closes with a discussion of various data structures used in this implementation.

Many architecture and dialog-related design decisions reached in this implementation were guided by the authors' prototyping with a cross section of potential database builders/users. The approach therefore does not stick rigidly to algorithms. Specifically the authors found high utility for (1) **memory aids**, examples to help users relate abstract ideas to the real situation and (2) an **explicit context** for user action whenever necessary. These resulted in fewer "cross checks" on the integrity in user input and a major reduction in design time.

6.2 ARCHITECTURE OF THE SYSTEM

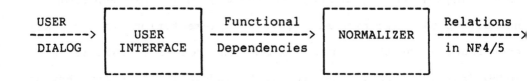

Figure 6.1

The system consists of two functionally distinct units - the User Interface and the Normalizer (Figure 6.1). The user interface is intelligent and it queries the user about his view of the enterprise and about data that are of interest to him. In the process the system infers any data dependencies and passes these on to the Normalizer. The Normalizer then analyzes these dependencies to produce a relation schema that eventually satisfies the fourth or fifth normal form.

6.3 USE OF PROLOG

Several factors governed the selection of a tool for this implementation. These factors are shown in Table 6.1. Certain symbolic manipulation requirements here could be met by logic programming tools alone. In this respect the task resembled that of constructing an expert system. Consequently, several AI programming tools were examined (see Table 6.2). ES shell EASE,

PC Scheme and TURBO Prolog came very close to meeting the requirements at hand. Choice of EASE was subsequently rejected because of its immediate non-availability. PC Scheme was deemed not sufficiently suitable for a dialog-based program: TURBO Prolog offered better screen control and input/output facility. Prototyping led to TURBO Prolog being finally selected as the vehicle for this implementation.

TURBO Prolog was eventually able to provide several additional advantages, as follows.

i)   Because of the list data structure, no storage space requirements are to be specified at the time of writing the program in TURBO Prolog.

ii) Prolog supports a dynamic database, which is stored in the memory along with the program. This is considerably more efficient than reading data from a file stored on a disk.

iii) Prolog code is very compact because a function can be used in more than one way.

iv) The backtracking mechanism of Prolog is a powerful aid for generating loops--a dearly needed logic programming artifact.

TABLE 6.1

CRITERIA FOR THE SELECTION OF TOOL FOR IMPLEMENTATION

User Considerations:

*   should be easily accessible (preferably be personal computer-based)

*   should support interactive screen control so that a friendly interface may be developed.

Implementation Considerations:

*   should be efficient in symbolic manipulation (most of time the system will operate on attribute names, which are symbols)

*   should support set operations (for easy implementation of normalization algorithms)

*   should efficiently perform logical procedures

*   should permit dialogue-based programming

TABLE 6.2

**VARIOUS ALTERNATIVES EXPLORED FOR SELECTION OF
A TOOL FOR IMPLEMENTATION**

a) **PC Scheme Version 3.0**

* a dialect of LISP developed at MIT

* available on IBM PCs.

* optimizes between memory requirement and speed

* supports graphics and windowing

b) **Expert System (ES) Shell-EASE**

* a product in the Personal Consultant Series of
Texas Instruments

* available on IBM PCs

* written in PC Scheme

* can read dBASE files and has access to DOS

* its code can be back compiled to C

c) **Micro PROLOG Version 2.2**

* a product of Expert Systems Ltd., Oxford, U.K.

* available on IBM PCs

* very poor environment for program development (for
example, no inbuilt editor)

* poor inbuilt functions for file handling and
input/output

d) **Expert System Shell VIDHI**

* developed by the Computer Science and Engineering department of IIT Kanpur

* interface with LISP but available only on DEC-1090

* good for logic/dialogue; poor screen control

e) **LISP**

* very good for set operations

* low level language, and many basic functions have to be written before a useful system can be built

* poor user interface and screen control

f) **TURBO Prolog Version 1.10**

* quick running version of Prolog created by Borland International Inc.

* available on IBM PCs

* has a user-friendly environment which facilitates quick program development

* contains an assortment of inbuilt functions for screen control and input-output handling

6.4 USER INTERFACE (UI) DEVELOPMENT

The design of UI aimed at retaining syntax and style natural to a common user so he can easily describe his environment of interest. Two specific design issues were faced in this process:

i) Visual Display Design: This should ensure that the communication from the user to the system (and vice-versa) is efficient.

ii) Dialog Design: The nature of the dialog should assure that right questions are posed to the user so that data dependencies (key inputs in normalization) can be systematically inferred.

6.4.1 Visual Display Design

In designing the display screens considerable use has been made of past research results available [3] in the area of user-interface design and our own prototyping of the system during its development with various levels of live users. For obvious reasons a strong effort was made to come up with an easy-to-use system, regardless of the complexity of the internal manipulations. The TURBO Prolog implementation itself spans over 40 pages of listing (Appendix B). The following general guidelines were observed:

A. **Provide sufficient Memory Aids.** Whenever the user is introduced to a new concept or terminology, its summary stays on the screen as the dialogue proceeds. This would give the user time to familiarize himself with the new concept he is expected to grasp and act on. For example, "data items" have been called "attributes" in the database design terminology used. Screen 3 introduces the user to the concept of attributes, and as the dialog proceeds, a summary of the definition stays on display till it is relevant, as shown on Screens 5-18.

B. **Aid the user in relating abstract ideas with real objects** by giving examples, so he can recognize the similar patterns or conditions (if any) in the personal design problem he is working with. The success of the dialog in inferring the dependencies would be governed by the efficacy with which the user could recognize relationships among the various data-items of his problem. The system aids the user in this process by providing him concrete examples. During prototyping it was noted that examples made recognition of (design inefficiency) patterns particularly easy for users. (see Screens 21-26).

C. Arrange the text on each presentation so as to **establish an explicit context for user action** A full use of colors and windows provided by TURBO Prolog was instrumental in achieving this goal. Each piece of logically different information is displayed in a different window to focus the user's attention. When the user is expected to relate information in different windows, he is assisted by a display of the points of focus (say a "Key") in identical colors.

6.4.2 Dialog Design

A functional dependency (FD) in a relation R, with attributes A_1, A_2, ... A_n, will be of the form:

$$X \dashrightarrow Y$$

where X and Y are the union of some of the A_i's. Constructing exhaustive combinations of attributes $[A_i]$ that might form X and Y and then checking for the dependence amongst them would be practically unfeasible. To tackle this problem an attempt has been made to exploit the natural structure of the information existing in the real world. The Entity-Relationship model, as proposed by Chen [6], is the basis of the approach followed in this work. According to Chen, semantically speaking there can be two types of functional dependencies:

a) FD's related to description of entities and relationships (including key dependencies), and

b) FD's related to entities in a relationship.

So instead of thinking of individual attributes, one may consider their aggregates, the entities, to trace dependencies. For instance, the moment the user specifies a key (cf. "surrogates" in the RM/T model [32]) for an entity, all dependencies which are the consequence of this key are specified in one shot. Special cases such as dependence on a part of the key and multivalued attributes would be handled separately. Inter-entity dependencies are inferred by making a note of the dependence between the keys of entities rather than exhaustively checking each of the attributes of these entities. This approach drastically cuts down the number of questions which would be posed to the user to infer the data dependencies.

The different stages through which the user-system dialog progresses are shown in Figure 6.2. The steps in each of these stages will be described now with reference to the appropriate interface screens in Appendix B.

A.   PRELIMINARIES

First, a few screens (Screen Numbers 1-4) introduce the user to the scope of the system and database design preliminaries.

B.   IDENTIFICATION OF ENTITIES

This stage is a bridge between a user's thinking and a database designer's terminology. A user interested in building a database is likely to think in terms of data files (Screen 5), which for a database designer are entities. The user is encouraged initially to classify meaning-wise and purpose-wise different (Screen 5) information into distinct files. In some cases these files may not be clearly identified by the user. In such an instance the user is first asked to enter the different attributes (data characteristics) he wishes to store (Screen 6). Then with the help of an example he is asked to sort these attributes into different logical groups. In each of these files or groups there is a possibility of further sorting the attributes into sub-groups. The groups/files identified in the first pass are termed strong entities whereas those identified in the second pass (i.e. subgroups) are termed weak entities.

Up to this point the user does not have to think specifically about any relationships because attributes which relate two entities will appear as characteristic in both the entities, signifying the relationship. If the user forgets to specify some relation, it is caught by the "loss-less join" check of the normalizer. If the user specifies some superfluous attributes in some relationship, they would be filtered out by the "minimal cover" check. In other words, the present approach exploits user knowledge about the semantic structure of the information the user wants to store and then process his inputs by an analytical procedure that would eliminate any redundant information.

C.   INPUT OF KEYS FOR ENTITIES

The system does the following:

i)   Explains to the user the concept of key (see Screen 15)

ii) Asks the user:

> Input the attributes that form the key,
  enter one attribute per line,
  when done, press return.

iii) Accepts the attributes which the user gives. Assures that
     at least one key is specified for each entity.

iv) Asserts (for internal processing) the dependency:

        Key attributes   ---> All non-key attributes in
        (As given in iii   that entity
         above)

D. DEPENDENCIES BASED ON A PART OF THE KEY

The system will:

i) Give an example where only a part of the key determines some of the non-key attributes (Screen 23).

ii) For each composite key (key with more than 1 attributes) ask

> For the composite key shown in the keys window, does there exist any dependent attribute that depends on only a part of this key (Y/N)?

iii) If the answer to (ii) is "no" then exit else goto Step (iv)

iv) Accept the part of the key and the attributes determined by it.

v) Assert (for internal processing) the dependency:

Part of the key --> Attributes dependent on it

E. MULTIVALUED ATTRIBUTES

The system proceeds to:

i) Give an example of multivalued attributes (Screen 21)

ii) For each key, ask the user:

> Is there any attribute which can take several values for the same value of the key (Y/N)?

iii) If the answer to ii) is "No" then exit, else goto step iv)

iv) Accept the multivalued attribute.

v) Ask the user:

> Is there any attribute whose value depends on the value of the attribute given above (Y/N)?

v) If the answer to iv) is "Yes", then accept the attributes dependent on the multivalued attribute (of Step iv). Assure that this dependent attribute is not contained in the key.

vi) Assert (for internal processing) a multivalued dependency:

Key -->> Multivalued attributes and the attributes
dependent on it.

F. DEPENDENCIES BASED ON NON-KEY ATTRIBUTES

i) For every key, display the key and non-key attributes in
parallel windows.

ii) Ask the user to familiarize himself with the windows. This
is done by displaying the message:

> Locate the window titled KEY ATTRIBUTES on the screen
(upper left corner) and also the window - NON KEY
ATTRIBUTES (above). Proceed with these two windows
in perspective.

iii) Ask the user:

> Normally a key attribute will determine the values of
non-key attributes. However, there may be
exceptions. In above windows, do you see a key
attribute whose value depends on some of the non-key
attributes (Y/N)?

iv) If the answer to iii) is "No", then exit else accept from
the user the concerned attributes.

v) Assert (for internal processing) the functional dependency:

nonkey attribute --> key attribute (as input in iv)

6.5 NORMALIZER

Algorithms used in the normalizer (Screens 27 and 28) employ the
information obtained by UI. The Normalizer (Figure 6.2) produces
a relation schema satisfying fourth normal form (see Screen 30).
Questions posed to the user to identify JDs to produce the fifth
normal form would be along the lines of Section 5.9.

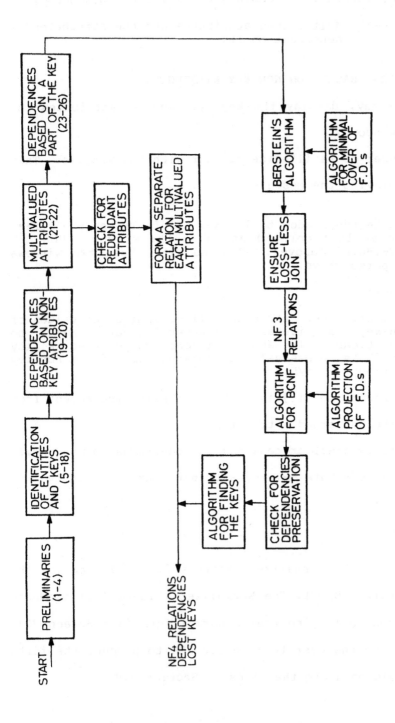

FIGURE 6.2: DETAILED FLOW CHART OF THE SYSTEM

(Numbers in brackets indicate the corresponding

Screen Numbers in Appendix B.)

6.6 Data Structures Used

Information provided by the user in response to the queries posed to him are stored by defining a separate TURBO Prolog database predicate for each different kind of information. The various predicates that were used are described below.

entity strong(A)   represents a strong entity whose name is A

entity weak(A,B)   represents a weak entity B, whose parent entity is A

attribute es(A,B)   represents an attribute B of the strong entity A

attribute ew(A,B,C)   represents an attribute C of the weak entity B, whose parent entity is A

attributes(L)   stores all the attributes in list L

key es(A,K)   Here, A is a one member list, where the element of A is the name of the entity for which K is the key. (The name had to be put in a list, because all the arguments in a compound object should be of the same data type and the general representation for a key is a list)

key ew(A,B,K)   Here again A and B are single member lists whose members are the names of the strong/weak entities with K as the key.

fd(A,B)   represents   a   functional   dependency:
                            A --> B

mvd(A,B)   represents   a   multivalued   dependency
                            A -->> B

fdmin(X,Y)   represents a functional dependency which
                            has been freed from redundancies

fdj(X,Y)   represents   equivalent   keys,   i.e.
the   dependencies: X --> Y and Y --> X

pj(L,M)   represents   a   projected   functional
                            dependency with   respect   to   the
                            relation under consideration

rel(L)   represents a relation with attributes L

key(K)   represents   the   key   K for the relation
                            under consideration

CHAPTER VII

CONCLUSIONS AND DIRECTIONS FOR FURTHER WORK

7.1 KEY RESULTS OF THIS WORK

i)   An interactive, expert framework that can automatically
     develop relational database schemas does seem feasible to
     build. This work presents a prototype.

ii) The present work shows that it is possible to assist the
     average database builder so he may develop good relational
     schemas in an unintimidating environment. The prototype
     presented here

         - assumes no formal knowledge of the database design
            principles on the part of the user, can act as an
            effective add-on design aid for a commercial DBMS or
            as a stand-alone system.

         - is dialog-based, which makes it easy to use, a
            familiar device increasingly being used for small
            scale data management/storage chores, and

         - can run on any IBM PC or similar machine.

iii) This work has combined the rigor of analytical design
     methods and the natural view in which a user is likely to
     describe or visualize objects and data-items around him.
     The result has been considerable gains in efficiency in
     developing the final design.

iv) This implementation has considered both multivalued dependencies and join dependencies explicitly, extending the domain of aided database design to a considerably larger set of data. A semantic-based approach has been emphasized here. This considerably reduces the total computational effort, particularly in the handling of MVDs and join dependencies.

v) Principles of good user-friendly interface design have been found to be immensely useful, and

vi) A new programming tool, TURBO Prolog, has been tested as a logic programming vehicle on a comprehensive task. In the authors' opinion its value in similar applications would be high.

7.2 DIRECTIONS FOR FURTHER WORK

i) The authors admit their own bias toward the relational model of data. Normalization, as stated in Section 4.2.9, assumes that non-key attributes in the database will be updated frequently. Hence an overall optimization with respect to storage space, access times and query processing may be brought into the design framework to help evaluate perhaps only partially normalized relations.

ii) Extensive field testing of the design proposed here will be necessary to further refine and perfect the user dialog before the system can become a stand-alone database design aid or the front end for a commercial DBMS.

iii) Graph-theoretic methods discussed by Yang [29] may be explored for an efficient algorithmic approach to develop the fourth normal form.

iv) Sufficiency conditions for the existence of MVDs or JDs do not appear to be available yet [33]. If these can be found, a user's assertion of MVDs or JDs can be verified.

The authors are pursuing these possibilities.

REFERENCES

1. Albano, A., Ed., Computer Aided Database Design - The DATAID Project, North Holland, Amsterdam (1985).

2. Alagic, S., Relational Database Technology, Springer-Verlag, New York (1986).

3. Bennette, J. L. (Ed.), Building Decision Support Systems, Addison-Wesley, Reading, MA (1983), pp. 41-64.

4. Bernstein, P.A., Synthesizing Third Normal Form Relations from Functional Dependencies, ACM Transactions on Database Systems, Vol 1., No 4 (December 1976), pp. 277-298.

5. Ceri, S., Gottlob, G., Normalization of Relations and Prolog, Comm. ACM, Vol. 29, No. 6 (June 1986), pp. 524-544.

6. Chen, P.P.S., The Entity-Relationship Model - Toward a Unified View of Data, ACM Transactions on Database Systems, Vol. 1, No. 1 (March 1976), pp. 9-36.

7. Codd, E.F., A Relational Model of Data for Large Shared Data Banks, Comm. ACM, Vol. 13, No. 6 (1970), pp. 377-387.

8. Date C.J., An Introduction to Database Systems, 3rd ed., Addison-Wesley, Reading, MA (1981).

9.   Fagin, R., Multivalued Dependencies and a New Normal Form
     for Relational Databases, ACM Transactions on Database
     Systems, Vol 2, No. 3 (Sep 1977), pp. 262-278.

10. Fagin R., Normal Forms and Relational Database Operators,
     Proc. ACM-SIGMOD, International Conference on Management of
     Data, Boston (May 1979), pp. 153-160.

11. Finkelstein, R., Pascal, F., SQL Database Management
     Systems, BYTE (January 1988), pp. 111-118.

12. Franklin, Jr., C., SQL Based Database Managers, BYTE
     (January 1988), pp. 121-130.

13. Gerritsen, R., The Relational and Network Models of
     Databases: Bridging the Gap, Second U.S.A. - Japan Computer
     Conference, 1975.

14. Gottlob, G., Computing Covers for Embedded Functional
     Dependencies, Internal Rep. 86-006. Dipartimentro di
     Electronica. Politecnico di Milano, Italy (submitted for
     publication.)

15. Gray, P., Logic Algebra and Databases, Ellis Horwood
     Limited, West Sussex (1985).

16. Kent, W., A Simple Guide to Five Normal Forms in Relational
     Database Theory, Comm. ACM, Vol. 26, No. 2 (February 1983),
     pp. 120-125.

17. Korth, H.F. and Silberschatz, A., Database System Concepts, McGraw-Hill Book Company, New York (1986).

18. Lien, Y.E., Hierarchical Schemata for Relational Databases, ACM Transactions on Database Systems, Vol. 6, No. 1 (March 1981), pp. 48-69.

19. Loizou, G., Thanish, P., Testing a Dependency Preserving Decomposition for Losslessness, Inf. Syst. Vol. 8, No. 1 (March 1983), pp. 25-28.

20. Lucchesi, C.L. and Osborne, S.L., Candidate Key for Relations, J. Comp. Syst. Sci., Vol. 17, No. 2 (October 1978), pp. 270-280.

21. Clocksin, W.F. and Mellish, C.S., Programming in Prolog, 3rd ed., Springer-Verlag Berlin, Heidelberg (1987).

22. Salzberg, B. J., Third Normal Form Made Easy, SIGMOD Record, Vol. 15, No.4 (December 1986), pp. 2-17.

23. Salzberg, B. J., An Introduction to Relational Database Design, Academic Press College Division, London (1986).

24. Spiegler, I., Automating Database Construction, Database, Vol. 14, No.3 (Spring 1983), pp. 21-29.

25. Teory, T.J., Dangqing, Y and Fry, J.P., A Logical Design Methodology for Relational Databases using Extended Entity-Relationship Model, Computing Surveys, Vol. 18, No.2 (June 1986).

26. Townsend, C., Introduction to TURBO Prolog, Sybex, Inc., Berkeley, CA (1986).

27. Tsou, D.M., Fischer, P.C., Decomposition of a Relation Scheme into Boyce-Codd Normal Form, ACM-SIGACT, 14, 3 (Summer 1982), pp. 23-29.

28. Ullman J.D., Principles of Database Systems, 2nd ed., Computer Science Press, Rockville, MD (1982).

29. Yang, C. C., Relational Databases, Prentice-Hall, Englewood Cliffs, NJ (1986).

30. Yao, S. Bing, (Ed.), Principles of Database Design, Vol. 1, Prentice-Hall, Englewood Cliffs, NJ (1985).

31. Chen & Associates, Inc., ER-Designer, Baton Rouge, LA, 1987.

32. Date, C.J., An Introduction to Database Systems, Vol II, Addison-Wesley, Reading, MA (1983).

33. Jajodia, S., Recognizing Multivalued Dependencies given FDs, The Computer Journal, Vol. 29, No. 5 (1986).

34. Smith, H.C., Database Design: Composing Fully Normalized Tables from a Rigorous Dependency Diagram, Comm. ACM, Vol. 28, No. 8 (August 1985), pp. 826-838.

APPENDIX A: A QUICK TOUR OF TURBO PROLOG

WHAT IS TURBO PROLOG?

PROLOG is an acronym for programming in logic. It was created in 1972 by the Faculty of Sciences, Luminy, in Marseilles, France. Prolog as described in Clocksin and Mellish' book, "Programming in Prolog", which is generally known as C&M Prolog, is widely accepted as the standard version of Prolog. TURBO Prolog, created by Borland Inc., is an IBM PC implementation of Prolog. This creation is a fast running version of Prolog which is both a subset and a superset of C&M Prolog. The key features of this implementation of Prolog are described in this Appendix.

PROGRAMMING IN PROLOG

Programming in Prolog consists of the following:

- Declaring some facts about objects and their relationships,
- Defining some rules about these objects and their relationships, and
- Asking questions (in the form of "goals") about these objects and their relationships.

The notions of facts, rules and goals may be stated as follows.

FACTS

- Facts define relationships among objects. For example, a fact may be stated as

      teaches(smith, math)

  which means that there is a relationship "teaches" between objects "smith" and "math".
- The order of objects (smith, math) is important in stating a fact for the correct interpretation of that fact.
- The name of a fact is called a predicate and the objects involved in the predicate are called arguments. In the above example, "teaches" is a predicate and "smith" and "math" are the arguments.
- A collection of facts is called a database. A typical Prolog database is shown below.

      teaches(smith,math)
      teaches(schriber,electronics)
      teaches(prabhakar,prolog)
      teaches(barua,unix)
      teaches(smith,lisp)

Figure A1: A TYPICAL PROLOG DATABASE

GOALS

A goal has the same form as a fact. Whenever a goal is posed,

Prolog searches through its database to check if the goal is true or false. This is done as follows. Two facts match if their predicates as well as the corresponding arguments are identical. If a match is found, Prolog comes back with the answer "true". Otherwise it returns "false". For example, in reference to the database of Figure A1, one may ask: teaches(smith,math). Prolog will respond "true".

RULES

Rules may be compared to IF-THEN statements of conventional programming languages. In Prolog terminology, rules are generalized statements about different objects and their relationships. For example, the relationship "taught" may imply the following.

Smith has taught anyone whose department is math and who has credited OR. This relationship may be generalized into a rule:

> Smith has taught X, where department of X is math and X has credited OR.

This generalized rule may be written in Prolog as

> taught(smith,x):- dept(x,math), credits(x,or)

One may easily note that the above rule has two parts: the **head** taught(smith,x) and the **body** dept(x,math), credits(x,or).

The comma between goals dept and credits denotes the conjunction. The comma implies that both goals must be satisfied for the overall goal to succeed (i.e. be true). In general, the body of a rule will be a conjunction of subgoals. The :- notation implies that the left hand side is true **if** the right hand side is true.

CLAUSES

The difference between a fact and a rule is that a fact does not have subgoals. A "clause" in Prolog is a general term for a fact or a rule. In the example of Figure A1, "taught" and "dept" are both clauses.

VARIABLES

Variables allow us to pose generalized goals. For example, if we wish to find which courses are taught by Smith, then instead of taking each possible subject and trying it to match it with the facts in the database, a generalized goal may be posed as

        teaches(smith,X)

Note here the use of upper case X, which denotes a variable. On encountering this goal Prolog will search its database and will give a list of all "X" values in the database that satisfy this goal, as follows.

        X = math
        X = lisp

At any time variables may be "instantiated" (bound to a certain value, e.g. statistics) or "uninstantiated" (not bound to any particular values).

BACKTRACKING

In Prolog, each goal keeps its own "place marker" in the database. For example, in attempting to check the following goal (to be true or false)

    teaches(smith,X), credits(barua, X)

Prolog starts with an attempt to satisfy the first (sub)goal. If this first goal is in the database, Prolog will mark the place of this match in the database and then try to match the second goal from the start of the database. If the second goal fails, Prolog will go back to the place of last instantiation of X, i.e. the place marker of the first goal and start searching through the remainder of the database for another match.

If another match to the first goal is found, Prolog will attempt to satisfy the second goal again with this second instantiated value for X, from the start of the database (see Figure A2).

Thus in a chain of goals, if any one goal fails, Prolog backtracks to the previous goal and tries to prove it again with another variable binding (instantiation). Prolog moves relentlessly forward and backward through the conditions, trying every available binding in an attempt to get the goal to succeed in as many ways as possible. The solution is displayed as a list.

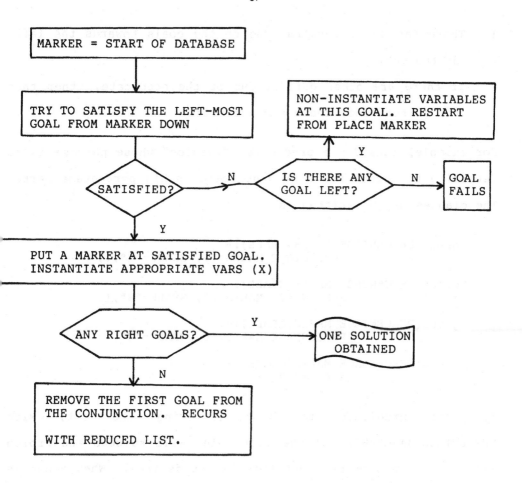

Figure A2:   BACKTRACKING MECHANISM IN PROLOG

CONTROL OF BACKTRACKING USING "CUT"

The primary purpose of "cut" is to prevent or stop backtracking

based on a specified condition.   The cut predicate is specified

as an exclamation mark (!).   It has no arguments and it always

succeeds.   One it succeeds, two things happen:

1. There can be no backtracking on the goals towards the left of the cut.

2. If there are other definitions of the predicate, other than the current one, these are not tried.

For example, consider a predicate "division" whose purpose is to determine the grade for a student based on his percentage marks. The clauses may be written as

```
grade(PERCENTAGE MARKS,GRADE):-
          PERCENTAGE MARKS>75, GRADE="A",!.

grade(PERCENTAGE MARKS,GRADE):-
          PERCENTAGE MARKS>60, GRADE="B",!.

grade(PERCENTAGE MARKS,GRADE):-
          PERCENTAGE MARKS>50, GRADE="C",!.

grade(PERCENTAGE MARKS,GRADE):-
          GRADE="F".
```

If this predicate is tried (ignoring the cut) with PERCENTAGE MARKS=80, all the four rules will succeed and Prolog will give four answers. But this is not desired. When a cut is placed in the first rule, the moment that rule is satisfied (i.e. PERCENTAGE MARKS>75) no further definitions are tried.

This is one way of using the cut. There are many other ways in which a cut may be used to control backtracking in Prolog.

DATA TYPES IN TURBO PROLOG

The basic data type in Prolog is a "term". Figure A3 identifies the different types which a term can take.

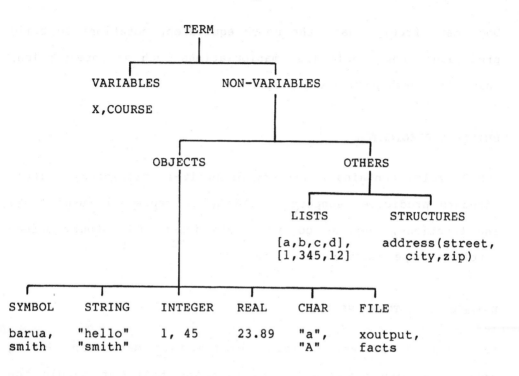

Figure A3:   BASIC DATA TYPES IN TURBO-PROLOG

LISTS

A list is an ordered sequence of terms. The components of a list
should be of the same data type. Examples of valid lists are
name, numbers, etc., where

        name=[smith,barua,codd]
        numbers=[1,2,25]

A list can be written in several alternate ways, by showing its
head and tail. For example, for list "name" one may have
equivalent lists:

        name=[smith,barua,codd]
        name=[smith¶[barua,codd]]
        name=[smith¶[barua¶[codd]]]

One may freely use the above equivalent notations to build predicates for basic list manipulations such as intersection, union, membership functions, etc.

BUILT-IN PREDICATES

TURBO Prolog contains a variety of built-in predicates. These standard predicates support a variety of repeatedly used tasks and functions, such as control, data input and output, screen handling, type conversions, etc.

DATABASES IN TURBO PROLOG

As mentioned earlier, a Prolog program is a database; Prolog acts as a very powerful query language that can handle the contents of this database. For instance, Prolog permits the selection of facts from a database. The program, however, is a static database. This implies that the database does not change with time. Once a Prolog program has been compiled, the knowledge in this database is frozen.

Prolog also has a dynamic database in which facts related to the current problem being solved are stored. This dynamic database is stored in memory along with the static database. The dynamic database can be saved to disk using the **save** predicate and read back using the **consult** predicate.

THE GENERAL STRUCTURE OF A TURBO PROLOG PROGRAM

The four sections in a TURBO Prolog program are as follows:

DOMAINS

data type declarations

DATABASE

predicates of dynamic database should be
defined here

PREDICATES

every predicate must be declared in
this section

CLAUSES

contain facts and rules

TURBO PROLOG PROGRAMMING ENVIRONMENT

TURBO Prolog has a user friendly environment with bouncing bar
menus. This is an interactive support that makes program
development fast. A display shows the environment screen.
Various menu options are as follows:

RUN	For running a program
COMPILE	For compiling a program
EDIT	To enter the editor
OPTIONS	To select compiler options (produce OBJ/EXE files)
FILES	File operations such as copy, rename, delete, etc.
SETUP	To change window sizes, colors, directories, etc.
QUIT	To quit the programming environment.

In the display, the editor window shows a predicate that will check the membership of an element in a list. When it is run (after compilation, as shown in the message window), the dialog window is activated. Goals may now be posed and solutions obtained as shown. The trace window would show a step by step progress of execution if desired.

SCREEN 1

PRELIMINARIES

| Files in a computer database are similar to paper files | except | that data is stored on magnetic media rather than on paper. |

In a database the different pieces of related information are grouped at one place. For example, a database may contain :

Roll No	Name	Class	Home Town
8678	Kasturi	M.Tech.	Madras
8760	Vijay	B.Tech.	Delhi

The individual data items in a database (Roll No, Name, etc.) are called attributes.

Press any key to continue ......

SCREEN 2

PRELIMINARIES

| Files in a computer database are similar to paper files | except | that data is stored on magnetic media rather than on paper. |

Soon, You will be asked some questions regarding the attributes (i.e. data items) that will appear in your database.

You should answer these questions thinking as if you are building ordinary paper files for storing data.

Press any key to continue ......

SCREEN 3

```
┌─────────────────────────────────────────────────────────────────┐
│ ┌───────Attributes───────────┐                                   │
│ │data items  to be stored     │                                  │
│ └─────────────────────────────┘                                  │
│              ┌────────────────────────────────────────┐          │
│              │                                          │         │
│              │  As you start the process of building    │        │
│              │  your database you may already have a     │        │
│              │  good idea about the data files  you      │        │
│              │  would like to have.                      │        │
│              │                                           │        │
│              │                                           │        │
│              │  For example, for a inventory manage-     │        │
│              │  ment database, you might have :          │        │
│              │                                           │        │
│              │       - a master file  of parts           │        │
│              │       - a master file of vendors          │        │
│              │                                           │        │
│              └───────────────────────────────────────────┘       │
│  ┌──────────────────────────DIALOG───────────────────────────┐   │
│  │ >  Can you already foresee the data files you will need (Y/N) ?N│
│  │                                                             │   │
│  └─────────────────────────────────────────────────────────────┘ │
└─────────────────────────────────────────────────────────────────┘
```

SCREEN 4

```
┌────────────────────────────────┬─────ATTRIBUTES IN FILE: ────────┐
│ ┌───────Attributes───────────┐ │ mech_no                          │
│ │data items  to be stored     │ │ skll_no                         │
│ └─────────────────────────────┘ │ skll_cat                        │
│                                  │ mech_name                       │
│                                  │                                 │
│                                  │                                 │
│                                  │                                 │
│                                  └─────────────────────────────────│
│                                  ┌──────────────DIALOG─────────────│
│                                  │ > Input the attributes you wish to store│
│                                  │   Give one attribute per line ...│
│                                  │   At end press Return           │
│                                  │ > MECH_NO                       │
│                                  │ > SKLL_NO                       │
│                                  │ > SKLL_CAT                      │
│                                  │ > MECH_NAME                     │
│                                  │ > MECH_AGE                      │
└────────────────────────────────┴─────────────────────────────────┘
```

SCREEN 5

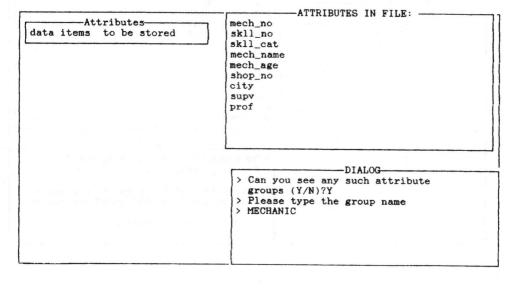

```
   ┌──────Attributes──────┐        ┌──────ATTRIBUTES IN FILE:──────┐
   │ data items  to be stored │      mech_no
   └──────────────────────┘        skll_no
                                    skll_cat
                                    mech_name
                                    mech_age
                                    shop_no
                                    city
   ┌─────EXAMPLE OF GROUPS─────┐    supv
                                    prof
     In a STUDENT database  with
     attributes :

     Name, Rollno, Class, Street,
     City, Zip                    ┌──────────DIALOG──────────┐
                                  > If you can now 'group' the above
     we might have the following    attributes  in some logical way,
     logical groups:                that would  reduce the number of
                                    questions  you  will  need  to
     GROUP 1:  Name, Rollno, Class  answer in this dialog
     GROUP 2:  Street, City, Zip    (see example)

                                    Press any key to continue ...
```

SCREEN 6

```
   ┌──────Attributes──────┐        ┌──────ATTRIBUTES IN FILE:──────┐
   │ data items  to be stored │      mech_no
   └──────────────────────┘        skll_no
                                    skll_cat
                                    mech_name
                                    mech_age
                                    shop_no
                                    city
                                    supv
                                    prof



                                  ┌──────────DIALOG──────────┐
                                  > Can you see any such attribute
                                    groups (Y/N)?Y
                                  > Please type the group name
                                  > MECHANIC
```

SCREEN 7

```
┌─────────Attributes─────────┐   ┌──────────ATTRIBUTES IN FILE: ──────────┐
│ data items  to be stored   │   │ mechanic                                │
└────────────────────────────┘   │ mech_no                                 │
                                  │ mech_name                               │
                                  │ mech_age                                │
                                  │ shop_no                                 │
                                  │                                         │
                                  │ skll_no                                 │
                                  │ skll_cat                                │
                                  │ city                                    │
                                  │ supv                                    │
                                  │ prof                                    │
                                  └─────────────────────────────────────────┘

                                  ┌─────────────────DIALOG─────────────────┐
                                  │ > For Group  : mechanic                 │
                                  │ > Enter one attribute per line ...      │
                                  │   When done, press Return               │
                                  │ > MECH_NO                               │
                                  │ > MECH_NAME                             │
                                  │ > MECH_AGE                              │
                                  │ > SHOP_NO                               │
                                  │ > SKLL_NO                               │
                                  └─────────────────────────────────────────┘
```

SCREEN 8

```
┌─────────Attributes─────────┐   ┌──────────ATTRIBUTES IN FILE: ──────────┐
│ data items  to be stored   │   │ shop        mech_age                    │
└────────────────────────────┘   │ shop_no     shop_no                     │
                                  │ city        skll_no                     │
                                  │ supv        prof                        │
                                  │                                         │
                                  │ skill                                   │
                                  │ skll_no                                 │
                                  │ skll_cat                                │
                                  │                                         │
                                  │ mechanic                                │
                                  │ mech_no                                 │
                                  │ mech_name                               │
                                  └─────────────────────────────────────────┘

                                  ┌─────────────────DIALOG─────────────────┐
                                  │ > To begin with we will make one file   │
                                  │   for each group.                       │
                                  │                                         │
                                  │   Attributes which are not in any group │
                                  │   will be put in a file named 'ungrouped'. │
                                  │ > Press any key to continue....         │
                                  └─────────────────────────────────────────┘
```

SCREEN 9

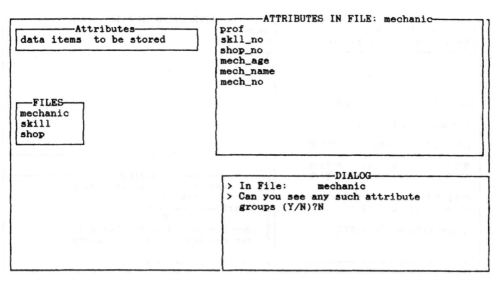

SCREEN 10

SCREEN 11

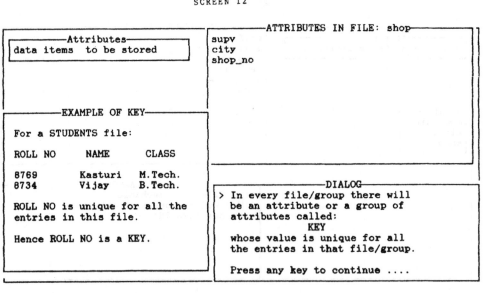

```
   ┌──────Attributes──────────┐      ┌────────ATTRIBUTES IN FILE: shop─────┐
   │ data items  to be stored │      │ supv                                │
   └──────────────────────────┘      │ city                                │
                                      │ shop_no                             │
                                      │                                     │
   ┌─FILES─┐                          │                                     │
   │mechanic│                         │                                     │
   │skill   │                         │                                     │
   │shop    │                         │                                     │
   └────────┘                         └─────────────────────────────────────┘

                                      ┌───────────────DIALOG────────────────┐
                                      │ >   ┌──NEXT STEP──────┐              │
                                      │     │EDIT THE DATA    │              │
                                      │     │PROCEED WITH DIALOG              │
                                      │     └──────────────────┘             │
                                      └─────────────────────────────────────┘
```

SCREEN 12

```
   ┌──────Attributes──────────┐      ┌────────ATTRIBUTES IN FILE: shop─────┐
   │ data items  to be stored │      │ supv                                │
   └──────────────────────────┘      │ city                                │
                                      │ shop_no                             │
   ┌────────EXAMPLE OF KEY────────┐   │                                     │
   │ For a STUDENTS file:         │   │                                     │
   │                              │   │                                     │
   │ ROLL NO    NAME    CLASS     │   └─────────────────────────────────────┘
   │ 8769     Kasturi  M.Tech.    │   ┌───────────────DIALOG────────────────┐
   │ 8734     Vijay    B.Tech.    │   │ > In every file/group there will    │
   │                              │   │   be an attribute or a group of     │
   │ ROLL NO is unique for all the│   │   attributes called:                │
   │ entries in this file.        │   │            KEY                      │
   │                              │   │   whose value is unique for all     │
   │ Hence ROLL NO is a KEY.      │   │   the entries in that file/group.   │
   │                              │   │                                     │
   └──────────────────────────────┘   │   Press any key to continue ....    │
                                       └─────────────────────────────────────┘
```

SCREEN 13

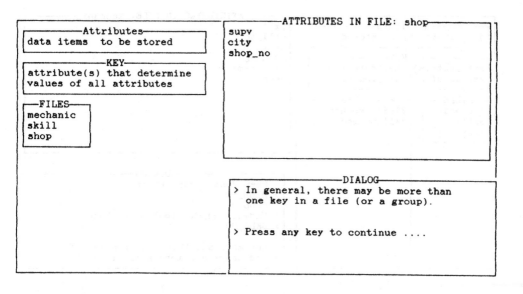

```
┌────────────────────────────────┐  ┌──────ATTRIBUTES IN FILE: shop──────┐
│ ┌──────Attributes──────────┐   │  │ supv                               │
│ │ data items  to be stored │   │  │ city                               │
│ └──────────────────────────┘   │  │ shop_no                            │
│ ┌───────────KEY───────────┐    │  │                                    │
│ │ attribute(s) that determine │ │  │                                    │
│ │ values of all attributes │   │  │                                    │
│ └──────────────────────────┘   │  │                                    │
│ ┌──FILES──┐                     │  │                                    │
│ │ mechanic│                     │  │                                    │
│ │ skill   │                     │  └────────────────────────────────────┘
│ │ shop    │                     │  ┌──────────────DIALOG──────────────┐
│ └─────────┘                     │  │ > In general, there may be more than │
│                                 │  │   one key in a file (or a group).   │
│                                 │  │                                     │
│                                 │  │ > Press any key to continue ....    │
│                                 │  │                                     │
└────────────────────────────────┘  └─────────────────────────────────────┘
```

SCREEN 14

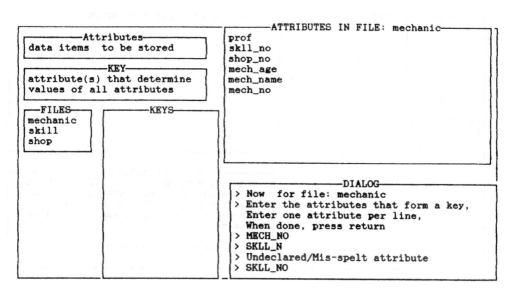

```
┌────────────────────────────────┐  ┌──────ATTRIBUTES IN FILE: mechanic──────┐
│ ┌──────Attributes──────────┐   │  │ prof                                   │
│ │ data items  to be stored │   │  │ skll_no                                │
│ └──────────────────────────┘   │  │ shop_no                                │
│ ┌───────────KEY───────────┐    │  │ mech_age                               │
│ │ attribute(s) that determine │ │  │ mech_name                              │
│ │ values of all attributes │   │  │ mech_no                                │
│ └──────────────────────────┘   │  │                                        │
│ ┌──FILES──┐  ┌────KEYS────┐     │  │                                        │
│ │ mechanic│  │            │     │  │                                        │
│ │ skill   │  │            │     │  └────────────────────────────────────────┘
│ │ shop    │  │            │     │  ┌──────────────DIALOG──────────────┐
│ └─────────┘  │            │     │  │ > Now  for file: mechanic         │
│              │            │     │  │ > Enter the attributes that form a key, │
│              │            │     │  │   Enter one attribute per line,   │
│              │            │     │  │   When done, press return         │
│              │            │     │  │ > MECH_NO                         │
│              │            │     │  │ > SKLL_N                          │
│              │            │     │  │ > Undeclared/Mis-spelt attribute  │
│              │            │     │  │ > SKLL_NO                         │
└──────────────┴────────────┘     │  └───────────────────────────────────┘
```

SCREEN 15

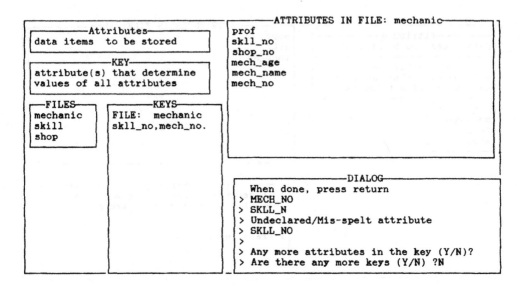

SCREEN 16

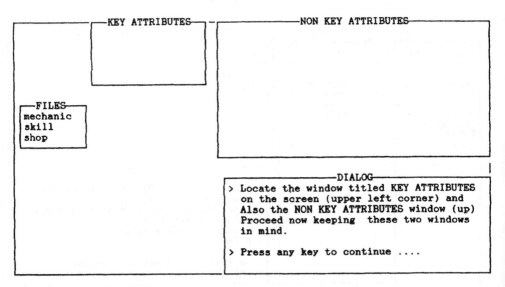

SCREEN 17

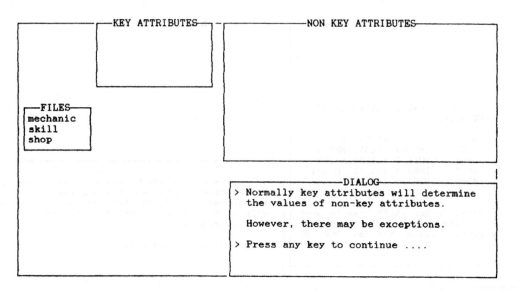

SCREEN 18

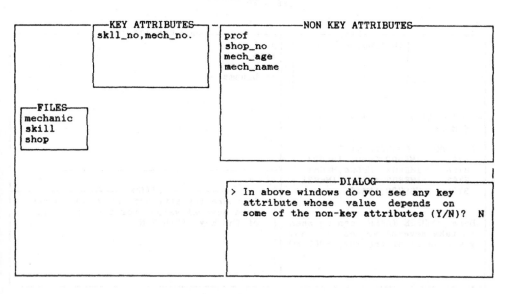

SCREEN 19

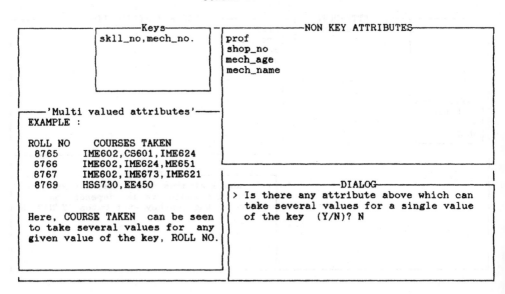

```
                                        ┌─────────NON KEY ATTRIBUTES─────────┐
┌──────────────────────────┐           │                                     │
│                          │           │                                     │
│                          │           │                                     │
│                          │           │                                     │
│  ──'Multi valued attributes'──      │                                     │
│  EXAMPLE :               │           │                                     │
│                          │           │                                     │
│  ROLL NO    COURSES TAKEN│           └─────────────────────────────────────┘
│   8765   IME602,CS601,IME624        ┌─────────────────────────────────────┐
│   8766   IME602,IME624,ME651        │              ──DIALOG──             │
│   8767   IME602,IME673,IME621       │> Now we need to know which among the │
│   8769   HSS730,EE450    │           │  attributes listed can take several  │
│                          │           │  values  for any given value of the key
│                          │           │  (see example).                      │
│  Here, COURSE TAKEN  can be seen    │                                      │
│  to take several values for  any    │> Press any key to continue ....      │
│  given value of the key, ROLL NO.   │                                      │
│                          │           │                                      │
└──────────────────────────┘           └─────────────────────────────────────┘
```

SCREEN 20

```
          ┌──────Keys──────┐           ┌─────────NON KEY ATTRIBUTES─────────┐
┌─────────│ skll_no,mech_no.│──────    │ prof                                │
│         │                 │          │ shop_no                             │
│         │                 │          │ mech_age                            │
│         │                 │          │ mech_name                           │
│         └─────────────────┘          │                                     │
│  ──'Multi valued attributes'──      │                                     │
│  EXAMPLE :               │           │                                     │
│                          │           │                                     │
│  ROLL NO    COURSES TAKEN│           │                                     │
│   8765   IME602,CS601,IME624        │                                     │
│   8766   IME602,IME624,ME651        │                                     │
│   8767   IME602,IME673,IME621       └─────────────────────────────────────┘
│   8769   HSS730,EE450    │           ┌─────────────────────────────────────┐
│                          │           │              ──DIALOG──             │
│  Here, COURSE TAKEN  can be seen    │> Is there any attribute above which can
│  to take several values for  any    │  take several values for a single value
│  given value of the key, ROLL NO.   │  of the key  (Y/N)? N               │
│                          │           │                                      │
└──────────────────────────┘           └─────────────────────────────────────┘
```

SCREEN 21

```
┌──────────────────Keys──────┐   ┌────────NON KEY ATTRIBUTES────────┐
│         shop_no.            │   │ supv                             │
│                            │   │ city                             │
│                            │   │                                  │
│                            │   │                                  │
│                            │   │                                  │
└────────────────────────────┘   │                                  │
┌───────Example of part key──────┐│                                  │
│                               ││                                  │
│ Roll No   Name  Course  Grade ││                                  │
│                               │└──────────────────────────────────┘
│  1267     ATUL  CADS     A    │┌──────────────DIALOG──────────────┐
│  1267     ATUL  DPS      B    ││ > Here we want to see if there are │
│  1267     ATUL  OR       C    ││   some attributes which depend on  │
│  1270     JOY   CADS     C    ││   only a part of the key (see example).│
│  1270     JOY   DPS      B    ││                                  │
│                               ││ > Press any key to continue ...   │
│ Key  is  (Roll No, Course)    ││                                  │
│ Name depends on only a part   ││                                  │
│ of the key, i.e.  Roll No.    ││                                  │
└───────────────────────────────┘└──────────────────────────────────┘
```

SCREEN 22

```
┌──────────────────KEYS──────┐   ┌────────NON KEY ATTRIBUTES────────┐
│      For Key :              │   │ prof                             │
│      skll_no,mech_no.       │   │ shop_no                          │
│                            │   │ mech_age                         │
│                            │   │ mech_name                        │
│                            │   │                                  │
└────────────────────────────┘   │                                  │
┌───────Example of part key──────┐│                                  │
│                               ││                                  │
│ Roll No   Name  Course  Grade ││                                  │
│                               ││                                  │
│  1267     ATUL  CADS     A    ││                                  │
│  1267     ATUL  DPS      B    │└──────────────────────────────────┘
│  1267     ATUL  OR       C    │┌──────────────DIALOG──────────────┐
│  1270     JOY   CADS     C    ││ > For the Key shown in KEYS window:│
│  1270     JOY   DPS      B    ││                                  │
│                               ││   Is there any attribute which is affected│
│ Key  is  (Roll No, Course)    ││   by only a part of the key (Y/N)?Y│
│ Name depends on only a part   ││                                  │
│ of the key, i.e.  Roll No.    ││                                  │
└───────────────────────────────┘└──────────────────────────────────┘
```

SCREEN 23

```
┌─────────────────KEYS──────────┐ ┌──────────NON KEY ATTRIBUTES──────────┐
│         For Key :             │ │ prof                                  │
│         skll_no,mech_no.      │ │ shop_no                               │
│                               │ │ mech_age                              │
│                               │ │ mech_name                             │
│                               │ │                                       │
│                               │ │                                       │
│   ──Example of part key───    │ │                                       │
│                               │ │                                       │
│  Roll No   Name  Course Grade │ │                                       │
│                               │ │                                       │
│   1267     ATUL   CADS    A   │ │                                       │
│   1267     ATUL   DPS     B   │ └───────────────DIALOG─────────────────┤
│   1267     ATUL   OR      C   │ │  Is there any attribute which is affected
│   1270     JOY    CADS    C   │ │  by only a part of the key (Y/N)?Y    │
│   1270     JOY    DPS     B   │ │ > Please enter the part key attributes│
│                               │ │   one by one. When done, press Return │
│   Key  is  (Roll No, Course)  │ │ > MECH_NO                             │
│   Name depends on only a part │ │ >                                     │
│   of the key, i.e.  Roll No.  │ │ > Any more attributes in part key (Y/N)?N
└───────────────────────────────┘ └───────────────────────────────────────┘
```

SCREEN 24

```
┌─────────────────KEYS──────────┐ ┌──────────NON KEY ATTRIBUTES──────────┐
│         For Key :             │ │ prof                                  │
│         skll_no,mech_no.      │ │ shop_no                               │
│                               │ │ mech_age                              │
│                               │ │ mech_name                             │
│                               │ │                                       │
│                               │ │                                       │
│   ──Example of part key───    │ │                                       │
│                               │ │                                       │
│  Roll No   Name  Course Grade │ │                                       │
│                               │ │                                       │
│   1267     ATUL   CADS    A   │ │                                       │
│   1267     ATUL   DPS     B   │ └───────────────DIALOG─────────────────┤
│   1267     ATUL   OR      C   │ │ > Please enter the part key attributes│
│   1270     JOY    CADS    C   │ │   one by one. When done, press Return │
│   1270     JOY    DPS     B   │ │ > MECH_NO                             │
│                               │ │ >                                     │
│   Key  is  (Roll No, Course)  │ │ > Any more attributes in part key (Y/N)?N
│   Name depends on only a part │ │ > Please type the affected attribute  │
│   of the key, i.e.  Roll No.  │ │ > MECH_NAME                           │
│                               │ │ > Any more such attributes (Y/N)?Y    │
└───────────────────────────────┘ └───────────────────────────────────────┘
```

SCREEN 25

```
────────────────NORMALIZING────────────────
> Retracting FD: ["mech_no"] -> ["mech_name"]
> Closure of LHS: ["mech_no","mech_age","shop_no","city","supv"]
> Does not contain RHS, Asserting again
> Retracting FD: ["shop_no"] -> ["city"]
> Closure of LHS: ["shop_no","supv"]
> Does not contain RHS, Asserting again
> Retracting FD: ["shop_no"] -> ["supv"]
> Closure of LHS: ["shop_no","city"]
> Does not contain RHS, Asserting again
> Retracting FD: ["skll_no"] -> ["skll_cat"]
> Closure of LHS: ["skll_no"]
> Does not contain RHS, Asserting again
> Retracting FD: ["skll_no","mech_no"] -> ["prof"]
> Closure of LHS: ["skll_no","mech_no","skll_cat","mech_name","mech_age","shop
_no","supv","city"]
> Does not contain RHS, Asserting again
> Redundant F.D's eliminated

> Loss-less join guaranteed
> Eliminating redundant relations
> 3rd NF obtained
> Press any key to continue ....
```

SCREEN 26

```
────────────────NORMALIZING────────────────
> 3rd NF obtained
> Press any key to continue ....
> Decomposing into BCNF the relation :  skll_no,mech_no,prof.
> Finding Projections
> Decomposed relation: skll_no,mech_no,prof.

> Decomposing into BCNF the relation :  skll_no,skll_cat.
> Finding Projections
> Decomposed relation: skll_no,skll_cat.

> Decomposing into BCNF the relation :  shop_no,supv,city.
> Finding Projections
> Decomposed relation: shop_no,supv,city.

> Decomposing into BCNF the relation :  mech_no,mech_name,mech_age,shop_no.
> Finding Projections
> Decomposed relation: mech_no,mech_name,mech_age,shop_no.

> Checking for dependency preservation
> Final filing scheme will be written to a file - 'OUTPUT',
  which can be printed using 'TYPE' command

> Press any key to continue ....
```

SCREEN 27

OUTPUT Notes

RELATION SCHEME IN FOURTH NORMAL FORM

ATTRIBUTES IN THE RELATION:
mech_no, mech_name, mech_age, shop_no.

KEYS:
mech_no.

ATTRIBUTES IN THE RELATION:
shop_no, supv, city.

KEYS:
shop_no.

—Scroll   PgUp—PgDn—Page   F1-Print page   F2-Print all

SCREEN 28

OUTPUT Notes

ATTRIBUTES IN THE RELATION:
skll_no, skll_cat.

KEYS:
skll_no.

ATTRIBUTES IN THE RELATION:
skll_no, mech_no, prof.

KEYS:
skll_no, mech_no.

—Scroll   PgUp—PgDn—Page   F1-Print page   F2-Print all

APPENDIX C

TURBO PROLOG PROGRAM LISTING

There are two types of files in this software:

i) Files with extensions '.txt'
ii) Files with extension '.pro'

'.txt' Files

These files contain text (such as definitions, examples, etc.)
which is to be displayed during the dialog.

There are 13 '.txt' files. These are listed below:

```
INSIGNIA TXT
TITLE    TXT
SCREEN1A TXT
SCREEN1B TXT
SCREEN1C TXT
OPEN_SCR TXT
SCREEN2A TXT
SCREEN2B TXT
SCREEN2C TXT
KEYS_DEF TXT
KEYS_EG  TXT
MVD_EG   TXT
PARTFD   TXT
```

The listing of these files is embedded in the listing of '.pro'
files.   Each file appears at the place where it is called by the
TURBO-PROLOG code.

'.pro' Files

These files contain the TURBO PROLOG code.

There are 6 '.pro' files. These are listed below:

UTILITY.PRO   Contains utility predicates for standard list
                operations,   such   as: union,   intersection,
                subtraction, etc.

SCREENS.PRO   Contains predicates for performing standard screen
                functions, such as: display of lists, display of
                attributes, etc..

INPFILE.PRO   Predicates in this section let the user input the data-items he wants to store in the database to be designed.

FDS.PRO   Predicates in this section conduct that part of the dialog which infers the functional dependencies from the user.

UI.PRO   Main program for the user interface. Master control of the dialog resides with the predicates in this file.

NORM.PRO   Predicates in this file implement the normalization algorithms.

STEPS FOR COMPILING THE PROGRAM:

1.   Check that all '.pro' and '.txt' files as listed above are in the same directory.

2.   Enter the TURBO-PROLOG environment (version 1.00). Set the default directories same as the directory in which all your '.pro' and '.txt' files are stored.

3.   Load the file : UI.PRO and compile using 'OBJ' option (For details refer pp. 202 of reference [26].

4.   Load the file : NORM.PRO and compile using 'OBJ' option.

5.   Create a small '.BAT' file named 'NORMEX.BAT' with following DOS commands:

```
echo off
ui
norm
echo on
```

6.   Quit the TURBO-PROLOG environment.

7.   Ensure that TURBO-PROLOG libraries :

```
PROLOG.OBJ
INIT.OBJ
```

are in the same directory in which the '.OBJ' files generated in step 3 & 4 are placed. Also the MS-DOS linker 'LINK.COM' and a batch file PLINK.BAT (which comes with TURBO-PROLOG) should be in the same directory

8.   Link the compiled modules using the commands:

```
plink ui
plink normex
```

This should create two files : ui.exe and norm.exe.

9.   You can run the program by typing 'normex' on the terminal.

STEPS FOR MAKING CHANGES IN THE PROGRAM:

1.   Depending on the nature of the change, and using the
description of '.pro' files given above, trace the file in which
the concerned predicate is likely to appear.

2.   Using the 'comments' given in that file (of step 1) trace
the section of interest.

3.   Trace the execution, starting from the top level predicate
and reach the point of your interest. Now you can make the
changes you desire.

```
/*****************************************************************************/
/*                                                                         */
/*                     LISTING OF VARIOUS FILES                            */
/*                                                                         */
/*                                                                         */
/* Each '.pro' file has various sections, each section beginning           */
/* with predicate declarations. Following have been specified for          */
/* each of section:                                                        */
/*                                                                         */
/*                                                                         */
/*   Purpose                Purpose/Role of the section                    */
/*   Top-level Predicate    The  predicate  which  controls the            */
/*                          flow of execution in that section              */
/*   Screen Numbers         Screen  Numbers  (of Appendix B) to            */
/*                          which this section corresponds                 */
/*                                                                         */
/*                                                                         */
/*****************************************************************************/
```

```
/*********************************************************************/
/*                                                                 */
/*              FILE         :    UI.PRO                            */
/*                                                                 */
/*              Main    program   for   the   user                 */
/*              interface.    Master control of                    */
/*              the   dialog   resides   with the                  */
/*              predicates in this file.                           */
/*                                                                 */
/*********************************************************************/


code=8000
DOMAINS

        list=symbol*
        file=output

DATABASE

        entity_strong(symbol)
        attribute_es(symbol,symbol)
        all_files(list)
        nfiles(integer)
        entity_weak(symbol,symbol)
        attribute_ew(symbol,symbol,symbol)
        key_es(list,list)
        key_ew(list,list,list)
        fd(list,list)
        fdmin(list,list)
        mvd(list,list)
        fdj(list,list)
        pj(list,list)
        attributes(list)
        key(list)
        user(string)
        schema_nf3(list)
        schema_bcnf(list)
        dep_preserved(string)


include "utility.pro"
include "screens.pro"
include "fds.pro"
include "inpfile.pro"
```

```
/*******************************************************************/
/*                                                               */
/*      PURPOSE:               GIVES THE USER AN OPTION  TO REVISE */
/*                             OLD   DESIGN                       */
/*                                                               */
/*      TOP LEVEL PREDICATE:   inputdata_where1                  */
/*                                                               */
/*      SCREEN  NUMBERS:       No corresponding screen numbers in */
/*                             Appendix B                        */
/*                                                               */
/*******************************************************************/


PREDICATES

        inputdata_where1
        inputdata_where2
        inputdata_where
        savefds


CLAUSES

savefds:-
        clearwindow,
        write("> Saving the dialogue in file : "),
        user(X),
        write(X),nl,nl,
        write("> Please wait ...."),nl,nl,
        save(X),
        write("> Saving Complete, "),nl,nl,
        write("        Press a key to continue ...."),
        readchar(_),
        clearwindow.


inputdata_where:-
        makewindow(6,2,11,"DIALOG",14,2,10,70),
        write("> Give a name for the database you want to design: "),
        readln(FILE1),
        not(FILE1=""),
        asserta(user(FILE1)),
        clearwindow,
        write("> The data requirements you input during this dialog"),nl,
        write("  will be stored.   This will allow you to revise the"),nl,
        write("  design on some later date, if the need arises."),nl,nl,
        write("> Press any key to continue ...."),
        readchar(_),
        removewindow,
        screen2,
        inputdata,
        !.

inputdata_where:-
        removewindow,
        inputdata_where.
```

```
inputdata_where2:-
        write("> Enter the old design name :   "),
        readln(X),
        consult(X),
        !,
        asserta(user(X)),
        removewindow,
        makewindow(4,0,0,"",7,1,3,3),
        makewindow(5,52,7,"ATTRIBUTES",0,34,14,45),
        makewindow(3,2,11,"DIALOG",15,35,10,45),
        display_files,
        shiftwindow(3),
        nextstep.

inputdata_where2:-
        write("> No such design name exists"),nl,nl,
        write("> Do you want to input again (Y/N)? "),
        readln(ANS),
        upper_lower("Y",ANS),nl,nl,
        !,
        inputdata_where2.

inputdata_where2:-
        removewindow,
        inputdata_where.

inputdata_where1:-
        makewindow(6,2,11,"DIALOG",14,2,10,70),
        clearwindow,
        write("> Do you wish to revise an old design (Y/N) ? "),
        readln(ANS),
        upper_lower("Y",ANS),nl,nl,
        inputdata_where2,
        !.

inputdata_where1:-
        removewindow,
        inputdata_where.
```

```
/*******************************************************************************/
/*                                                                             */
/*      PURPOSE:                MASTER CONTROL OF THE DIALOG                    */
/*                                                                             */
/*      TOP LEVEL PREDICATE     go                                             */
/*                                                                             */
/*      SCREEN NUMBERS:         1-26                                           */
/*                                                                             */
/*******************************************************************************/

PREDICATES
        main_control
        go
        start


CLAUSES

main_control:-
        start,
        introduction,
        inputdata_where1,
        savefds,
        keys,
        nextstep,
        fds,
        save("pipe").

start:-
        asserta(all_files([])),
        asserta(nfiles(0)).

go:-
        main_control.

goal
        go.
```

```
/*************************************************************************/
/*                                                                     */
/*              FILE        :        NORM.PRO                           */
/*                                                                     */
/*              The predicates in   this   file                        */
/*              implement various normalization                        */
/*              algorithms.                                            */
/*                                                                     */
/*************************************************************************/


code=6000
DOMAINS

        list=symbol*
        file=output

DATABASE

        entity_strong(symbol)
        attribute_es(symbol,symbol)
        all_files(list)
        nfiles(integer)
        entity_weak(symbol,symbol)
        attribute_ew(symbol,symbol,symbol)
        key_es(list,list)
        key_ew(list,list,list)
        fd(list,list)
        fdmin(list,list)
        mvd(list,list)
        fdj(list,list)
        pj(list,list)
        attributes(list)
        key(list)
        user(string)
        schema_nf3(list)
        schema_bcnf(list)
        dep_preserved(string)

include "utility.pro"
include "displays.pro"
```

```
/*****************************************************************************/
/*                                                                         */
/*    PURPOSE:                TO FIND THE CLOSURE OF A SET                  */
/*                            OF ATTRIBUTES                                 */
/*                                                                         */
/*    TOP LEVEL PREDICATE     closure                                      */
/*                                                                         */
/*****************************************************************************/
```

PREDICATES

```
        closure(string,list,list)
        getfd(string,list,list)
```

CLAUSES

```
        /*      closure(string,list1,list2)     */
        /* Computes closure (list1) of attributes (list2)      */
        /* w.r.t. f.d's denoted by string.                     */

        closure(S,A,APLUS):-
                getfd(S,LHS,RHS),
                subset(LHS,A),
                not (subset (RHS,A)),
                union(TEMP,A,RHS),
                closure(S,TEMP,APLUS),
                !.

        closure(_,A,APLUS):-
                !,
         APLUS=A.


        /*      getfd(list1,list2)       */
        /*      Picks up one fd from the list of f.d's  */

        getfd("F",LHS,RHS):-
                fd(LHS,RHS).

        getfd("F",LHS,RHS):-
                fdmin(LHS,RHS).

        getfd("P",LHS,RHS):-
                pj(LHS,RHS).
```

```
/**********************************************************************/
/*                                                                  */
/*      PURPOSE:                    TO COMPUTE THE MINIMAL COVER  OF  */
/*                                  A SET OF FUNCTIONAL DEPENDENCIES  */
/*                                                                  */
/*      TOP LEVEL PREDICATE:        minimum_cover                    */
/*                                                                  */
/*                                                                  */
/**********************************************************************/
```

PREDICATES

```
        reducefds
        reducelhs1
        reducelhs2(list,list,list)
        minimum_cover
```

CLAUSES

```
        /* Eliminates redundant f.d's */

        reducefds:-
                write("> Eliminating Redundant F.D.'s"),
                nl,
                fail.

        reducefds:-
                fd(LHS,RHS),
                not(fdj(LHS,_)),
                retract(fd(LHS,RHS)),
                write("> Retracting FD: ",LHS," -> ",RHS),nl,
                closure("F",LHS,LHSPLUS),
                write("> Closure of LHS: ",LHSPLUS),nl,
                not (subset(RHS,LHSPLUS)),
                write("> Does not contain RHS, Asserting again"),nl,
                asserta(fdmin(LHS,RHS)),
                fail.

        reducefds:-
                retract(fdmin(X,Y)),
                asserta(fd(X,Y)),
                fail.

        reducefds:-
                write("> Redundant F.D's eliminated"),
                nl,nl.

        /*  Minimise the number of attributes on Left Hand Side */

        reducelhs1:-
                fd(LHS,RHS),
                write("> FD: ",LHS," -> ",RHS),nl,
                reducelhs2(LHS,RHS,REDLHS),
                not(equal(LHS,REDLHS)),
                retract(fd(LHS,RHS)),
                asserta(fd(REDLHS,RHS)),
                fail.
```

```
reducelhs1:-
        !,
        write("> LHS minimised"),
        nl,nl.

reducelhs2(LHS,RHS,REDLHS):-
        member(ELEM,LHS),
        drop_elem(LHS,ELEM,LHSM1),
        closure("F",LHSM1,LHSM1PLUS),
        subset(RHS,LHSM1PLUS),
        !,
        reducelhs2(LHSM1,RHS,REDLHS).


reducelhs2(REDLHS,_,REDLHS).


minimum_cover:-
        reducelhs1,
        reducefds.
```

```
/**********************************************************************/
/*                                                                  */
/*      PURPOSE:                  TO PROJECT A SET OF FD'S ON TO     */
/*                                A SET OF ATTRIBUTES                */
/*                                                                  */
/*      TOP LEVEL PREDICATE:      pj1                               */
/*                                                                  */
/*                                                                  */
/**********************************************************************/

PREDICATES

        pj1(list)
        pj2(symbol)

CLAUSES

pj1(_):-
        retract(pj(_,_)),
        fail.

pj1(_):-
        fd(X,Y),
        asserta(pj(X,Y)),
        fail.

pj1(SET):-
        attributes(L),
        member(E,L),
        not (member(E,SET)),
        pj2(E),
        fail.

pj1(_).

pj2(E):-
        pj(LHS1,[E]),
        pj(LHS2,RHS2),
        member(E,LHS2),
        drop_elem(LHS2,E,TEMP),
        union(NEWLHS,TEMP,LHS1),
        asserta(pj(NEWLHS,RHS2)),
        fail.

pj2(E):-
        pj(LHS,RHS),
        member(E,LHS),
        retract(pj(LHS,RHS)),
        fail.

pj2(E):-
        pj(LHS,RHS),
        member(E,RHS),
        retract(pj(LHS,RHS)),
        fail.

pj2(_).
```

```
/************************************************************************/
/*                                                                    */
/*      PURPOSE:                    TO DETERMINE ALL THE KEYS OF A      */
/*                                  RELATION                           */
/*                                                                    */
/*      TOP LEVEL PREDICATE:        findallkeys                        */
/*                                                                    */
/*                                                                    */
/************************************************************************/

PREDICATES

        findkey(list,list)
        findallkeys
        knownkey(list)
        findnewkey(list)

CLAUSES

findkey(_,_):-
        retract(key(_)),
        fail.

findkey(REL,KEY):-
        mvd(X,Y),
        union(REL,X,Y),
        KEY=REL,
        asserta(key(KEY)),
        !.

findkey(REL,KEY):-
        reducelhs2(REL,REL,KEY),
        assertz(key(KEY)).

knownkey(K):-
        key(S),
        subset(K,S),
        !.

findnewkey(K):-
        pj(LHS,RHS),
        minus(RHS,K,Z),
        union(S,LHS,Z),
        not (knownkey(S)),
        asserta(key(S)),
        findnewkey(S).

findallkeys:-
        key(K),
        findnewkey(K),
        fail.

findallkeys.
```

```
/**********************************************************************/
/*                                                                    */
/*      PURPOSE:                    TO OBTAIN THE THIRD NORMAL FORM    */
/*                                  USING BERNSTEIN'S ALGORITHM        */
/*                                                                    */
/*      TOP LEVEL PREDICATE:        nf3                                */
/*                                                                    */
/*                                                                    */
/**********************************************************************/

PREDICATES

        combinefds
        makerel
        nf3
        elem_containedins
        eqvkeys
        collectalleqv(list,list,list)
        collectalleqv1(list,list,list)
        collectalleqv2(list,list,list)
        alreadyexists(list)

CLAUSES

        combinefds:-
                fd(LHS1,RHS1),
                write("> FD: ",LHS1," -> ",RHS1),nl,
                fd(LHS2,RHS2),
                equal(LHS1,LHS2),
                not(equal(RHS1,RHS2)),
                write("> FD: ",LHS2, " -> ",RHS2),nl,
                union(RHS,RHS1,RHS2),
                retract(fd(LHS1,RHS1)),
                retract(fd(LHS2,RHS2)),
                write("> Combining to :"),nl,
                write("> FD: ",LHS1, " -> ",RHS),nl,nl,
                asserta(fd(LHS1,RHS)),
                !,
                combinefds.

        combinefds.
```

```
collectalleqv(LHS,A,R):-
        collectalleqv1(LHS,A,R1),
        collectalleqv2(LHS,R1,R).


collectalleqv2(LHS,A,R):-
        fd(LHS,RHS),
        union(Z1,LHS,RHS),
        union(R1,Z1,A),
        not(equal(R1,A)),
        !,
        collectalleqv(LHS,R1,R).

collectalleqv2(_,A,A).

collectalleqv1(LHS1,A,R):-
        fdj(LHS1,LHS2),
        retract(fdj(LHS1,LHS2)),
        retract(fdj(LHS2,LHS1)),
        !,
        collectalleqv1(LHS1,A,R1),
        collectalleqv2(LHS2,R1,R).

collectalleqv1(_,A,A).


alreadyexists(R):-
        schema_nf3(Z),
        equal(R,Z),
        !.

makerel:-
        fdj(LHS1,LHS2),
        retract(fdj(LHS1,LHS2)),
        retract(fdj(LHS2,LHS1)),
        collectalleqv(LHS1,[],R1),
        collectalleqv(LHS2,R1,R2),
        asserta(schema_nf3(R2)),
        fail.

makerel:-
        fd(LHS,_),
        collectalleqv2(LHS,[],R),
        not (alreadyexists(R)),
        asserta(schema_nf3(R)),
        fail.

makerel:-
        elem_containedins,
        fail.

makerel:-
        retract(schema_nf3([])),
        fail.

makerel:-
        mvd(X,Y),
        union(Z,X,Y),
        asserta(schema_nf3(Z)),
        fail.
```

```
makerel.

elem_containedins:-
        schema_nf3(Z1),
        schema_nf3(Z2),
        subset(Z2,Z1),
        not (subset(Z1,Z2)),
        retract(schema_nf3(Z2)),
        fail.

elem_containedins:-
        !.

eqvkeys:-
        fd(LHS1,_),
        fd(LHS2,_),
        not (equal (LHS1,LHS2)),
        closure("F",LHS1,LHS1P),
        closure("F",LHS2,LHS2P),
        subset(LHS2,LHS1P),
        subset(LHS1P,LHS2P),
        not (fdj(LHS1,LHS2)),
        writelist_hz(LHS1),
        write("  and   "),
        writelist_hz(LHS2),
        write(" are equivalent keys."),nl,
        asserta(fdj(LHS1,LHS2)),
        asserta(fdj(LHS2,LHS1)),
        fail.

eqvkeys.

nf3:-
        consult("pipe"),
        findall(X,attribute_es(_,X),L1),
        findall(Y,attribute_ew(_,_,Y),L2),
        union(L,L1,L2),
        asserta(attributes(L)),
        fail.

nf3:-
        write("> Finding minimum cover"),nl,
        minimum_cover,
        fail.

nf3:-
        write("> Finding equivalent keys"),nl,
        eqvkeys,
        write("> Finding cover for the second time"),nl,
        minimum_cover,
        fail.

nf3:-
        makerel,
        fail.
```

```
nf3:-
        attributes(L),
        findkey(L,K),
        asserta(schema_nf3(K)),
        write("> Loss-less join guaranteed"),nl,
        fail.

nf3:-
        write("> Eliminating redundant relations"),nl,
        elem_containedins,
        fail.

nf3:-
        write("> 3rd NF obtained"),
        nl,
        write("> Press any key to continue ...."),nl,
        readchar(_),
        !.
```

```
/**********************************************************************/
/*                                                                  */
/*      PURPOSE:                   TO CHECK FOR THE PRESERVATION OF  */
/*                                 DEPENDENCIES                      */
/*                                                                  */
/*      TOP LEVEL PREDICATE:       fdlost1                          */
/*                                                                  */
/*                                                                  */
/**********************************************************************/

PREDICATES

        fdlost1
        fdlost2(list,list)
        isitlost(list,list,list)

CLAUSES

fdlost1:-
        write("> Checking for dependency preservation"),nl,
        asserta(dep_preserved("YES")),
        fd(X,Y),
        fdlost2(X,Z),
        isitlost(X,Y,Z),
        fail.

fdlost1.

fdlost2(X,Z):-
        schema_bcnf(R),
        intersect(X,R,XIR),
        closure("F",XIR,XIRPLUS),
        intersect(XIRPLUS,R,ADD),
        union(ZTEMP,ADD,X),
        not (equal( ZTEMP,X)),
        !,
        fdlost2(ZTEMP,Z).

fdlost2(X,X).

isitlost(_,Y,Z):-
        subset(Y,Z),
        !.

isitlost(X,Y,_):-
        retract(dep_preserved(_)),
        asserta(dep_preserved("NO")),
        write(X),
        write("  --->>  "),
        write(Y),nl.
```

```
/***********************************************************************/
/*                                                                   */
/*      PURPOSE:                    TO OBTAIN BOYCE-CODD NORMAL FORM  */
/*                                                                   */
/*      TOP LEVEL PREDICATE:        bcnftop                          */
/*                                                                   */
/*                                                                   */
/***********************************************************************/


PREDICATES

        bcnftop
        bcnf(list)

CLAUSES

bcnf(REL):-
        write("> Finding Projections"),NL,
        pj1(REL),
        findkey(REL,_),
        findallkeys,
        fail.

bcnf(REL):-
        pj(X,Y),
        closure("P",X,XPLUS),
        not(subset(REL,XPLUS)),
        !,
        write("> BCNF violated, Decomposing the relation"),nl,
        union(Z,X,Y),
        asserta(schema_bcnf(Z)),
        write("> Decomposed relation: "),
        writelist_hz(Z),nl,
        minus(NEWREL,REL,Y),
        bcnf(NEWREL).

bcnf(REL):-
        write("> Decomposed relation: "),
        writelist_hz(REL),nl,
        asserta(schema_bcnf(REL)).

bcnftop:-
        schema_nf3(REL),
        write("> Decomposing into BCNF the relation :   "),
        writelist_hz(REL),
        bcnf(REL),
        fail.

bcnftop:-
        fdlost1,
        !.
```

```
/*********************************************************************/
/*                                                                   */
/*      PURPOSE:                  PRINTING OF OUTPUTS                 */
/*                                                                   */
/*      TOP LEVEL PREDICATE:      writerel                           */
*/
  /*                                                                 */
  /*******************************************************************/

PREDICATES
        writerel(string)
        writerela(list)
        writekeys

CLAUSES


writekeys:-
        write("KEYS: "),nl,
        fail.

writekeys:-
        key(K),
        writelist_infile(output,K),
        fail.

writekeys:-
        nl,nl,nl.

writerela(X):-
        pj1(X),
        findkey(X,_),
        findallkeys,
        write("ATTRIBUTES IN THE RELATION:"),nl,
        writelist_infile(output,X),nl,
        writekeys.

writerel("BCNF"):-
        schema_bcnf(R),
        writerela(R),
        fail.

writerel("NF3"):-
        schema_nf3(R),
        writerela(R),
        fail.

writerel(_).
```

```
/*************************************************************************/
/*                                                                     */
/*      PURPOSE:                  MASTER CONTROL OF NORMALIZATION       */
/*                                                                     */
/*      TOP LEVEL PREDICATE:      normalize                            */
/*                                                                     */
/*                                                                     */
/*************************************************************************/

PREDICATES
        normalize
        print_output

CLAUSES

print_output:-
        write("> Final filing scheme will be written to a file -
            'OUTPUT',"),nl,
        write("  which can be printed using 'TYPE' command"),nl,nl,
        write("> Press any key to continue ...."),
        readchar(_),
        openwrite(output,"OUTPUT"),
        writedevice(output),nl,nl,nl,
        fail.

print_output:-
        dep_preserved("NO"),
        write("              RELATION SCHEME IN THIRD NORMAL FORM"),NL,NL,
        nl,nl,
        writerel("NF3"),nl,nl,nl,nl,
        fail.

print_output:-
        write("              RELATION SCHEME IN FOURTH NORMAL FORM"),NL,NL,
        nl,nl,
        writerel("BCNF"),nl,nl,
        fail.

print_output:-
        dep_preserved("NO"),
        write("Data Dependencies Lost in the Decomposition"),nl,
        fdlost1,
        fail.

print_output:-
        closefile(output),
        writedevice(screen),
        fail.

print_output:-
        file_str("OUTPUT",B),
        write(B),
        nl,nl,
        write("> Press any key to continue ...."),NL,
        readchar(_).
```

```
normalize:-
        makewindow(1,78,7,"NORMALIZING",0,0,25,80),
        nf3,
        bcnftop,
        fdlost1,
        print_output.

goal
        normalize.
```

```
/**************************************************************************/
/*                                                                      */
/*              FILE        :    SCREENS.PRO                             */
/*                                                                      */
/*              Predicates in this file perform some standard screen    */
/*              functions, such as, displaying lists, displaying file   */
/*              names, displaying attributes, etc.                      */
/*                                                                      */
/**************************************************************************/



/**************************************************************************/
/*                                                                      */
/*    PURPOSE:                   TO DISPLAY OPENING SCREENS AND          */
/*                               INTRODUCE THE USER TO THE              */
/*                               PRELIMINARIES OF DATABASE DESIGN       */
/*                                                                      */
/*    TOP LEVEL PREDICATE        introduction                           */
/*                                                                      */
/*    SCREEN NUMBERS             1-4                                     */
/*                                                                      */
/**************************************************************************/

PREDICATES

        opening_screen
        screen1
        screen2
        zoom(integer,integer,integer,integer)
        wait(integer)
        insignia
        introduction

CLAUSES

/****************************************************/
/*                                                */
/*      FILE:   OPEN_SCR.TXT                       */
/*                                                */
/*                                                */
/*              Hello!                            */
/*                                                */
/*    We are here to assist  you in developing a  */
/*                                                */
/*              Filing Scheme                      */
/*                                                */
/*          for your database.                     */
/*                                                */
/*        Press any key to continue ....          */
/*                                                */
/****************************************************/

opening_screen:-
        makewindow(2,116,0,"",7,15,15,50),
        file_str("open_scr.txt",A),
        write(A),
        field_attr(6,17,13,79),
        readchar(_),
        removewindow.
```

```
/**********************************************************************/
/*                                                                  */
/*              FILE        :     UTILITY.PRO                        */
/*                                                                  */
/*              The predicates in   this   files                    */
/*              perform standard list operations                    */
/*              such as, union, intersection,etc.                   */
/*                                                                  */
/**********************************************************************/


predicates
        member(symbol,list)
        subset(list,list)
        union(list,list,list)
        minus(list,list,list)
        equal(list,list)
        drop_elem(list,symbol,list)
        nth_elemENT(integer,list,integer,symbol)

clauses

        /*      member(symbol,list)      */
        /*      checks the membership of symbol in the list      */

        Member(X,[X!_]).
        Member(X,[_!Tail]):-
                Member(X,Tail).

        /*      subset(list1,list2)      */
        /*      Checks to see whether list1 is a subset of list2 */

        subset([],_):-
                !.
        subset([HEAD!TAILA],B):-
                !,
                member(HEAD,B),subset(TAILA,B).

        /*      drop_elem(list1,symbol,list2)   */
        /*      subtracts symbol from list1 to give list2        */

        drop_elem([ELEM!REDLHS],ELEM,REDLHS):-
                !.
        drop_elem([A!LHS],ELEM,[A!REDLHS]):-
                drop_elem(LHS,ELEM,REDLHS).

        /*      union(list1,list2,list3          */
        /* Returns union (list1)  of two sets (list2 and list3) */

        union(A,A,[]):-!.
        union(A,[],A):-!.
        union([HEADA!TAILU],[HEADA!TAILA],B):-
                member(HEADA,B),
                !,
                drop_elem(B,HEADA,B1),
                union(TAILU,TAILA,B1).
        union([HEADA!TAILU],[HEADA!TAILA],B):-
                !,union(TAILU,TAILA,B).
```

```
        /*      minus(list1,list2,list3)        */
        /* Subtracts list3 from list2 to give list1 */

        minus(SET,SET,[]):-
                !.
        minus(SETDIFF,SETA,[HEADB|TAILB]):-
                drop_elem(SETA,HEADB,TEMP),
                minus(SETDIFF,TEMP,TAILB).

        /*      equal(list1,list2)      */
        /*      Checks equality of two lists list1 and list2    */

        equal(X,Y):-
                subset(X,Y),
                subset(Y,X),
                !.

        /*      nth_element(integer1,list,integer2,symbol)    */
        /*      Returns the position integer2, of the
                symbol in the list counting from integer1 */

        nth_element(IN,[HEAD|_],IN,HEAD):-
                !.

        nth_element(IN,[_|TAIL],N,X):-
                OUT=IN+1,
                nth_element(OUT,TAIL,N,X).

predicates
    intersect(list,list,list)
clauses

    intersect([],_,[]).
    intersect([H|T],Y,[H|T2]):-
        member(H,Y),!,intersect(T,Y,T2).
    intersect([_|T],Y,Z):- intersect(T,Y,Z).
```

```
/**************************************************************************
/*                                                                       *
/*              FILE          :      SCREENS.PRO                          *
/*                                                                        *
/*              Predicates in this file perform some standard screen      *
/*              functions, such as, displaying lists, displaying file     *
/*              names, displaying attributes, etc.                       */
/*                                                                        *
/**************************************************************************


/***********************************************************************/
/*                                                                     */
/*      PURPOSE:                 TO DISPLAY OPENING SCREENS AND         */
/*                               INTRODUCE THE USER TO THE              */
/*                                  PRELIMINARIES OF DATABASE DESIGN    *
/*                                                                     */
/*      TOP LEVEL PREDICATE      introduction                          */
/*                                                                     */
/*      SCREEN NUMBERS           1-4                                   */
/*                                                                     */
/***********************************************************************/

PREDICATES

        opening_screen
        screen1
        screen2
        zoom(integer,integer,integer,integer)
        wait(integer)
        insignia
        introduction

CLAUSES

/***************************************************/
/*                                                 */
/*      FILE:   OPEN_SCR.TXT                        */
/*                                                 */
/*                                                 */
/*                 Hello!                           */
/*                                                 */
/*    We are here to assist  you in developing a    */
/*                                                 */
/*                 Filing Scheme                    */
/*                                                 */
/*          for your database.                      */
/*                                                 */
/*          Press any key to continue ....          */
/*                                                 */
/***************************************************/

opening_screen:-
        makewindow(2,116,0,"",7,15,15,50),
        file_str("open_scr.txt",A),
        write(A),
        field_attr(6,17,13,79),
        readchar(_),
        removewindow.
```

```
/*************************************************************************/
/*                                                                     */
/*      FILE:    SCREEN1A.TXT                                          */
/*                                                                     */
/*                                                                     */
/* An  efficient database design assures that  only minimal effort and */
/* time are expended in storing, retrieving, revising and manipulating */
/* the information stored in the database.                             */
/*                                                                     */
/*                                                                     */
/* This   programme  uses Artificial Intelligence concepts to guide you */
/* to achieve  an  efficient  database design based on the  relational */
/* model of storing the data.                                         */
/*                                                                     */
/* Press  any key to continue ......                                   */
/*                                                                     */
/*                                                                     */
/*************************************************************************/
/*                                                                     */
/*      FILE:    SCREEN1B.TXT                                          */
/*                                                                     */
/*   In a database the different pieces of related information are     */
/*   grouped at one place.  For example, a database may contain :      */
/*                                                                     */
/*      Roll No       Name        Class           Home Town           */
/*      8678          Kasturi     M.Tech.         Madras              */
/*      8760          Vijay       B.Tech.         Delhi               */
/*                                                                     */
/*   The individual  data items in a database (Roll No, Name, etc.)    */
/*   are  called attributes.                                          */
/*                                                                     */
/*      Press  any key to continue ......                             */
/*                                                                     */
/*************************************************************************/
/*                                                                     */
/*      FILE:    SCREEN1C.TXT                                          */
/*                                                                     */
/*                                                                     */
/*   Soon, You will be asked some questions regarding the attributes   */
/*   (i.e. data items) that will appear in your database.              */
/*                                                                     */
/*                                                                     */
/*   You should answer these questions thinking as if you are building */
/*   ordinary paper files for storing data.                           */
/*                                                                     */
/*   Press  any key to continue ......                                 */
/*                                                                     */
/*************************************************************************/
```

```
screen1:-
        makewindow(1,15,15,"",0,0,25,80),
        cursor(2,36),
        write("except"),
        cursor(0,32),
        write("PRELIMINARIES"),
        makewindow(2,116,15,"",2,2,4,34),
        write(" Files in a computer database"),nl,
        write(" are similar to paper files"),
        makewindow(3,116,15,"",2,44,4,35),
        write(" that data is stored on magnetic"),
        write(" media rather than on  paper."),
        makewindow(5,2,15,"",8,2,16,76),
        window_attr(2),
        file_str("screen1a.txt",A),
        write(A),
        readchar(_),
        clearwindow,
        file_str("screen1b.txt",B),window_attr(2),
        write(B),
        field_attr(4,1,70,14),
        field_attr(9,16,11,11),
        readchar(_),
        clearwindow,
        file_str("screen1c.txt",C),
        write(C),
        readchar(_),
        removewindow,
        removewindow,
        removewindow,
        clearwindow,
        shiftwindow(1),
        makewindow(2,90,10,"Attributes",1,1,3,31),
        clearwindow,
        write("data items  to be stored").

/****************************************************/
/*                                                  */
/*      FILE:   SCREEN2A.TXT                         */
/*                                                  */
/*                                                  */
/*   As you start the process of building           */
/*   your database you may already have a           */
/*   good idea about the data files  you            */
/*   would like to have.                            */
/*   for example:                                   */
/*                                                  */
/*   For example, for a inventory manage-           */
/*   ment database, you might have :                */
/*                                                  */
/*        - a master file  of parts                 */
/*        - a master file of vendors                */
/*                                                  */
/****************************************************/
```

```
screen2:-
        makewindow(3,74,2,"",4,16,15,47),
        file_str("screen2a.txt",A),
        write(A),
        field_attr(3,23,11,79),
        field_attr(10,1,35,79),
        field_attr(11,1,35,79),
        fail.

screen2:-
        makewindow(6,2,11,"DIALOG",19,2,5,70),
        fail.

screen2.

wait(1000):-
        !.

wait(N):-
        NO=N+1,
        !,
        wait(NO).
```

```
/***********************************************************/
/*                                                       */
/*              FILE:    SCREEN2A.TXT                     */
/*                                                       */
/*   A TURBO-PROLOG IMPLEMENTATION OF NORMALIZATION       */
/*      ALGORITHMS IN RELATIONAL DATABASE DESIGN          */
/*                                                       */
/*                  Copyright                            */
/*              Vinay K Chaudhri                          */
/*              Tapan P. Bagchi                           */
/*                                                       */
/*                                                       */
/*   INDUSTRIAL AND MANAGEMENT ENGINEERING PROGRMME       */
/*              IIT KANPUR UP, 208016                     */
/*                                                       */
/***********************************************************/
```

```
zoom(_,_,X,_):-
        X>15,
        file_str("title.txt",A),
        write(A),
        !.


zoom(STXI,STYI,HTI,WIDTHI):-
        removewindow,
        makewindow(1,11,0,"",STXI,STYI,HTI,WIDTHI),
        STXO=STXI-1,
        STYO=STYI-5,
        HTO=HTI+2,
        WIDTHO=WIDTHI+10,
        wait(0),
        !,
        zoom(STXO,STYO,HTO,WIDTHO).

insignia:-
        file_str("insignia.txt",A),
        makewindow(2,12,0,"",0,0,25,80),
        write(A),
        makewindow(1,90,0,"",11,37,3,3),
        zoom(11,38,3,3),wait(-31999),wait(-31999),
        removewindow,
        removewindow,
        !.

introduction:-
        insignia,
        opening_screen,
        screen1.
```

```
/**********************************************************************/
/*                                                                    */
/*      PURPOSE:                     TO IMPLEMENT A POP UP MENU        */
/*                                                                    */
/*      TOP LEVEL PREDICATE          menu                             */
/*                                                                    */
/*      SCREEN NUMBERS               14                               */
/*                                                                    */
/**********************************************************************/

DOMAINS
  ROW,COL,LEN = INTEGER
  ST=string
  KEY     = cr ; esc ; break ; tab ; btab ; del ; bdel ; ins ;
              end ; home ; ftast(INTEGER) ; up ; down ; left ; right ;
              ctrlleft; ctrlright; ctrlend; ctrlhome; pgup; pgdn;
              chr(CHAR) ; otherspec

PREDICATES
  readkey(KEY)
  readkey1(KEY,CHAR,INTEGER)
  readkey2(KEY,INTEGER)

CLAUSES

  readkey(KEY):-readchar(T),char_int(T,VAL),readkey1(KEY,T,VAL).

  readkey1(KEY,_,0):-!,readchar(T),char_int(T,VAL),readkey2(KEY,VAL).
  readkey1(cr,_,13):-!.
  readkey1(esc,_,27):-!.
  readkey1(chr(T),T,_) .

  readkey2(up,72):-!.
  readkey2(down,80):-!.
  readkey2(ftast(N),VAL):-VAL>58,VAL<70,N=VAL-58,!.
  readkey2(otherspec,_).

/* menu(Line,Collum,Header,ListOfChoices,ChoiceNr)               */
/* The following keys can be used:                               */
/*      arrows up and down: select choice                        */
/*      cr and F10: activate choice                              */
/*      Esc: abort                                               */

PREDICATES
  maxlen(LIST,INTEGER,INTEGER) /* Find length of the longest string */
  listlen(LIST,INTEGER)                /* Find the length of a list  */
  writelist(INTEGER,INTEGER,LIST)      /* Used by the menu predicate */
  menu(ROW,COL,STRING,LIST,INTEGER)
  menu1(ROW,LIST,INTEGER,INTEGER,INTEGER)
  menu2(ROW,LIST,INTEGER,INTEGER,INTEGER,KEY)
```

```
clauses

  maxlen([H!T],MAX,MAX1):-
              ST=H,
              str_len(ST,LEN),
              LEN>MAX,!,
              maxlen(T,LEN,MAX1).

maxlen([_!T],MAX,MAX1):-maxlen(T,MAX,MAX1).

maxlen([],LEN,LEN).

listlen([],0).

listlen([_!T],N):-
              listlen(T,X),
              N=X+1.

writelist(_,_,[]).

writelist(LINE,LONGEST_CHOICE,[H!T]):-field_str(LINE,0,LONGEST_CHOICE,H),
              LINE1=LINE+1,writelist(LINE1,LONGEST_CHOICE,T).


menu(LINE,KOL,TXT,LIST,ACTUAL_CHOICE):-
              maxlen(LIST,0,LONGEST_CHOICE),
              listlen(LIST,LEN),NCHOICE=LEN,LEN>0,
              HH1=NCHOICE+2,HH2=LONGEST_CHOICE+2,
              makewindow(3,7,7,TXT,LINE,KOL,HH1,HH2),
              HH3=LONGEST_CHOICE,
              writelist(0,HH3,LIST),cursor(0,0),
              menu1(0,LIST,NCHOICE,LONGEST_CHOICE,CHOICE),
              ACTUAL_CHOICE=1+CHOICE,
              removewindow.

menu1(LINE,LIST,NCHOICE,LONGEST_CHOICE,CHOICE):-
              field_attr(LINE,0,LONGEST_CHOICE,112),
              cursor(LINE,0),
              readkey(KEY),
              menu2(LINE,LIST,NCHOICE,LONGEST_CHOICE,CHOICE,KEY).

menu2(_,_,_,_,-1,esc):-!.

menu2(LINE,_,_,_,CHOICE,ftast(10)):-!,CHOICE=LINE.

menu2(LINE,_,_,_,CHOICE,cr):-!,CHOICE=LINE.

menu2(LINE,LIST,NCHOICE,LONGEST_CHOICE,CHOICE,up):-
              LINE>0,!,
              field_attr(LINE,0,LONGEST_CHOICE,7),
              LINE1=LINE-1,
              menu1(LINE1,LIST,NCHOICE,LONGEST_CHOICE,CHOICE).

menu2(LINE,LIST,NCHOICE,LONGEST_CHOICE,CHOICE,down):-
              LINE<NCHOICE-1,!,
              field_attr(LINE,0,LONGEST_CHOICE,7),
              LINE1=LINE+1,
              menu1(LINE1,LIST,NCHOICE,LONGEST_CHOICE,CHOICE).

menu2(LINE,LIST,NCHOICE,LONGEST_CHOICE,CHOICE,_):-
              menu1(LINE,LIST,NCHOICE,LONGEST_CHOICE,CHOICE).
```

```
/********************************************************************/
/*                                                                  */
/*      PURPOSE:                TO DISPLAY ATTRIBUTES, FILES AND     */
/*                              KEYS                                 */
/*                                                                  */
/*      TOP LEVEL PREDICATES    display_files, display_attribs,     */
/*                              display_keys                        */
/*                                                                  */
/********************************************************************/
```

PREDICATES

```
    display_list(LIST,INTEGER,ROW,INTEGER,STRING,INTEGER,INTEGER)
    move_cursor(INTEGER,INTEGER,INTEGER,INTEGER)
    disp_list_col(INTEGER,INTEGER,LIST)
    writelist_hz(list)
    display_attribs(symbol)
    display_attribs_ew(symbol,symbol)
    display_files
    display_keys(symbol)
    display_keys_es1(symbol)
    display_keys_es2(symbol)
    display_keys_ew1(symbol,symbol)
    display_keys_ew2(symbol,symbol)
    writelist_infile(file,list)
    findall_att(symbol,symbol,list)
```

CLAUSES

```
    findall_att(FILE,"",ALL):-
        findall(P,attribute_es(FILE,P),ALL),
        !.

    findall_att(FILE,GROUP,ALL):-
        findall(P,attribute_ew(FILE,GROUP,P),ALL).

    display_list(LIST,WINDO_NO,LINE,COLUMN,HEADER,SCR_ATTRIB,FRAME_ATTRIB):-
                LONGEST_CHOICE=10,
                listlen(LIST,LEN),NCHOICE=LEN,LEN>0,
            HH1=NCHOICE+2,HH2=LONGEST_CHOICE+2,
                HH3=LONGEST_CHOICE,
                shiftwindow(WINDO_NO),
                removewindow,
                makewindow(WINDO_NO,SCR_ATTRIB,FRAME_ATTRIB,HEADER,
                           LINE,COLUMN,HH1,HH2),
                writelist(0,HH3,LIST).

    display_list(_,WINDO_NO,_,_,_,_,_):-
                shiftwindow(WINDO_NO),
                removewindow,
                makewindow(4,0,0,"",7,1,3,3).

    move_cursor(10,33,_,_):-
                cursor(11,32),
                write("SPACE FULL"),
                field_attr(11,32,10,67),
                shiftwindow(3),
                !,
```

```
move_cursor(11,X,O,Y):-
               Y=X+11,
               cursor(O,Y),
               !.

move_cursor(X,Y,P,Y):-
               P = X+1,
               cursor(P,Y),
               !.

 disp_list_col(_,_,[]):-
               !.

 disp_list_col(STY,STX,[HEAD!TAIL]):-
               write(HEAD),
               move_cursor(STY,STX,STYO,STXO),
               !,
               disp_list_col(STYO,STXO,TAIL).

 disp_list_col(_,_,_).

 writelist_hz([]):-
       cursor(X,Y),
       P=Y-1,
       cursor(X,P),
       write("."),
       nl,
       !.

writelist_hz([H!T]):-
       write(H),
       write(","),
       !,
       writelist_hz(T).

display_files:-
       shiftwindow(3),
       retract(all_files(_)),
       findall(X,entity_strong(X),FILE_LIST),
       asserta(all_files(FILE_LIST)),
       not(equal(FILE_LIST,[])),
       display_list(FILE_LIST,4,8,1,"FILES",74,15),
       shiftwindow(3),
       !.

display_files.


display_attribs_ew(_,GROUP):-
       shiftwindow(5),
       clearwindow,
       not (GROUP=""),
       write(GROUP),
       field_attr(0,0,10,79),nl,
       fail.
```

```
display_attribs_ew(FILE,GROUP):-
        findall_att(FILE,GROUP,ATTRIB_LIST),
        cursor(P,Q),
        disp_list_col(P,Q,ATTRIB_LIST),
        shiftwindow(3).

display_attribs(FILE):-
        all_files(LIST),
        nth_element(0,LIST,N,FILE),
        shiftwindow(4),
        field_attr(N,0,10,75),
        fail.

display_attribs(FILE):-
        shiftwindow(5),
        removewindow,
        concat("ATTRIBUTES IN FILE: ",FILE,X),
        makewindow(5,52,11,X,0,34,14,45),
        clearwindow,
        fail.

display_attribs(FILE1):-
        entity_weak(FILE1,EW),
        cursor(M,N),
        write(EW),
        field_attr(M,N,10,79),
        move_cursor(M,N,P,Q),
        findall(X,attribute_ew(FILE1,EW,X),ATTRIB_LIST),
        disp_list_col(P,Q,ATTRIB_LIST),
        cursor(X,Y),
        move_cursor(X,Y,_,_),
        fail.

display_attribs(FILE1):-
        findall(X,attribute_es(FILE1,X),REST),
        cursor(P,Q),
        disp_list_col(P,Q,REST),
        shiftwindow(3),
        fail.

display_attribs(_):-
        !.

display_keys(_):-
        shiftwindow(7),
        clearwindow,
        fail.

display_keys(FILE1):-
        entity_weak(FILE1,X),
        display_keys_ew1(FILE1,X),
        fail.

display_keys(FILE1):-
        display_keys_es1(FILE1),
        fail.


display_keys(_):-
        shiftwindow(3).
```

```
display_keys_ew1(FILE1,X):-
        key_ew([FILE1],[X],_),
        cursor(P,Q),
        write("Group: "),
        write(X),nl,
        field_attr(P,Q,18,26),
        !,
        display_keys_ew2(FILE1,X).

display_keys_ew1(_,_).

display_keys_ew2(FILE1,X):-
        key_ew([FILE1],[X],KEY1),
        writelist_hz(KEY1),
        fail.

display_keys_ew2(_,_).

display_keys_es1(FILE1):-
        key_es([FILE1],_),
        cursor(P,Q),
        write("FILE:  "),
        write(FILE1),nl,
        field_attr(P,Q,18,26),
        !,
        display_keys_es2(FILE1).

display_keys_es1(_).

display_keys_es2(FILE1):-
        key_es([FILE1],KEY1),
        writelist_hz(KEY1),
        fail.

display_keys_es2(_).


writelist_infile(FILE,[]):-
        filepos(FILE,-2,1),
        write("."),nl,
        !.

writelist_infile(FILE,[H!T]):-
        write(H),
        write(", "),
        !,
        writelist_infile(FILE,T).
```

```
/**********************************************************************/
/*                                                                    */
/*              FILE            :      INPFILE.PRO                     */
/*                                                                    */
/*              Predicates in   this   file let                       */
/*              the user        the user input the                    */
/*              data-items he wishes to store in                      */
/*              the database to be designed                           */
/*                                                                    */
/**********************************************************************/




/**********************************************************************/
/*                                                                    */
/*      PURPOSE:                   TO TRUNCATE THE ATTRIBUTE NAMES     */
/*                                 TO A LENGTH OF 10 CHARACTERS        */
/*                                                                    */
/*      TOP LEVEL PREDICATE        chop_name                          */
/*                                                                    */
/**********************************************************************/

PREDICATES

        chop_name(symbol,symbol)

CLAUSES

chop_name(A,A):-
        str_len(A,L),
        L<11,
        !.

chop_name(A,B):-
        frontstr(10,A,B,_).
```

```
/***********************************************************************/
/*                                                                   */
/*    PURPOSE:                 TO ACCEPT THE INPUT OF WEAK ENTITIES   */
/*                                                                   */
/*    TOP LEVEL PREDICATE      explaingroup                          */
/*                                                                   */
/*    SCREEN NUMBERS           7-10                                  */
/*                                                                   */
/***********************************************************************/


PREDICATES

        explaingroup(symbol)
        ask_groups_es(symbol)
        ask_groups_es1(symbol)
        ask_attrib_ew(symbol,symbol)
        ask_attrib_ew1(symbol,symbol)
        check_duplicate_group(symbol,symbol)
        check_null_group(symbol,symbol,list)
        check_name_attrib_ew1(symbol,symbol,symbol)
        editkeys_ew(symbol,symbol)

CLAUSES

/**************************************************/
/*                                              */
/*      FILE:   SCREEN2B.TXT                     */
/*                                              */
/*                                              */
/*      In a STUDENT database  with             */
/*      attributes :                            */
/*                                              */
/*      Name, Rollno, Class, Street,            */
/*      City, Zip                               */
/*                                              */
/*      we might have the following             */
/*      logical groups:                         */
/*                                              */
/*      GROUP 1:  Name, Rollno, Class           */
/*      GROUP 2:  Street, City, Zip             */
/*                                              */
/**************************************************/
```

```
/****************************************************/
/*                                                  */
/*       FILE:    SCREEN2C.TXT                       */
/*                                                  */
/*       If you can now 'group' the above           */
/*       attributes  in some logical way,           */
/*       that would  reduce the number of           */
/*       questions  you  will   need   to           */
/*       answer in this dialog                      */
/*       (see example)                              */
/*                                                  */
/*       Press any key to continue ...              */
/*                                                  */
/****************************************************/


explaingroup(FILE1):-
        clearwindow,
        file_str("screen2c.txt",C),
        write(C),
        makewindow(7,26,7,"EXAMPLE OF GROUPS",8,0,16,35),
        file_str("screen2b.txt",A),
        write(A),
        readchar(_),
        removewindow,
        shiftwindow(3),
        clearwindow,
        ask_groups_es(FILE1).

ask_groups_es(FILE1):-
        display_attribs(FILE1),nl,
        clearwindow,
        not (FILE1=""),
        write("> In File:      "),
        write(FILE1),
        field_attr(0,15,25,11),
        nl,fail.

ask_groups_es(FILE1):-
        write("> Can you see any such attribute "),nl,
        write("  groups (Y/N)?"),
        readln(ANS),
        upper_lower("Y",ANS),
        ask_groups_es1(FILE1).

ask_groups_es(_).


ask_groups_es1(FILE1):-
        write("> Please type the group name "),nl,
        write("> "),
        readln(NAMEU),
        not(NAMEU=""),
        upper_lower(NAMEU,NAMEL),
        chop_name(NAMEL,NAME),
        check_duplicate_group(FILE1,NAME),
        fail.
```

```
ask_groups_es1(FILE1):-
        write("> Any more groups (Y/N)? "),
        readln(ANS),
        upper_lower("Y",ANS),
        !,
        ask_groups_es1(FILE1).

ask_groups_es1(_).

check_duplicate_group(FILE1,NAME):-
        entity_weak(FILE1,X),
        X=NAME,
        write("> Duplicate names not allowed"),nl,
        !,
        ask_groups_es1(FILE1).

check_duplicate_group(FILE1,NAME):-
        asserta(entity_weak(FILE1,NAME)),
        ask_attrib_ew(FILE1,NAME).

editkeys_ew(FILE1,NAME):-
        key_es(_,_),
        !,
        clearwindow,
        write(">  For   file :   "),
        write(FILE1),nl,
        field_attr(0,15,25,11),
        cursor(PP,_),
        write(">  For group :   "),
        write(NAME),
        field_attr(PP,15,25,14),nl,
        ask_keys1(FILE1,NAME),
        clearwindow.

editkeys_ew(_,_).

ask_attrib_ew(FILE1,GROUP):-
        clearwindow,
        cursor(R,_),
        write("> For Group  : "),
        write(GROUP),nl,
        field_attr(R,15,25,14),
        write("> Enter one attribute per line ..."),nl,
        write("  When done, press Return"),nl,
        ask_attrib_ew1(FILE1,GROUP),
        fail.

ask_attrib_ew(FILE1,GROUP):-
        write("> Any more attributes (Y/N)? "),
        readln(ANS),
        upper_lower("Y",ANS),
        !,
        ask_attrib_ew(FILE1,GROUP).

ask_attrib_ew(FILE1,GROUP):-
        findall(X,attribute_ew(FILE1,GROUP,X),ATT_LIST),
        check_null_group(FILE1,GROUP,ATT_LIST),
        display_attribs(FILE1),
        editkeys_ew(FILE1,GROUP).
```

```
ask_attrib_ew1(FILE1,GROUP):-
        display_attribs(FILE1),
        write("> "),
        readln(NAMEU),
        not (NAMEU=""),
        upper_lower(NAMEU,NAMEL),
        chop_name(NAMEL,NAME),
        check_name_attrib_ew1(FILE1,GROUP,NAME),
        !,
        ask_attrib_ew1(FILE1,GROUP).

ask_attrib_ew1(_,_).

check_name_attrib_ew1(FILE1,GROUP,NAME):-
        retract(attribute_es(FILE1,NAME)),
        assertz(attribute_ew(FILE1,GROUP,NAME)),
        !.

check_name_attrib_ew1(FILE1,GROUP,NAME):-
        attribute_ew(FILE1,_,NAME),
        assertz(attribute_ew(FILE1,GROUP,NAME)),
        !.

check_name_attrib_ew1(_,_,_):-
        write("> Undeclared/Misspelt attribute"),nl,
        write("  Please check and input again"),nl,nl.

check_null_group(FILE1,GROUP,[]):-
        write("> Empty groups not accepted"),nl,nl,
        write("> Do you want to keep this group (Y/N)? "),
        readln(ANS),
        upper_lower("Y",ANS),
        !,
        ask_attrib_ew(FILE1,GROUP).

check_null_group(FILE1,GROUP,[]):-
        retract(entity_weak(FILE1,GROUP)),
        !.

check_null_group(_,_,_).
```

```
/***********************************************************************/
/*                                                                     */
/*    PURPOSE:                    TO ACCEPT THE INPUT OF STRONG ENTITIES */
/*                                                                     */
/*    TOP LEVEL PREDICATE         ask_filenames2                       */
/*                                                                     */
/***********************************************************************/


PREDICATES

        ask_file_names1
        ask_file_names2
        check_null_file1(symbol)
        check_null_file2(symbol,list)
        check_duplicate_file(symbol)
        ask_attribs_es1
        ask_attribs_es2(symbol)
        check_duplicate_attrib_es(symbol,symbol)
        editkeys_es(symbol)

CLAUSES

ask_attribs_es1:-
        entity_strong(FILE1),
        display_files,
        clearwindow,
        write("> Now For file: "),
        write(FILE1),nl,
        field_attr(0,15,25,11),
        write("  Enter one attribute per line ..."),nl,
        write("  When done, press Return"),nl,
        makewindow(5,52,7,"ATTRIBUTES",0,34,14,45),
        display_files,
        display_attribs(FILE1),
        shiftwindow(3),
        ask_attribs_es2(FILE1),
        fail.

ask_attribs_es1.

ask_attribs_es2(FILE1):-
        write("> "),
        readln(AU),
        not (AU=""),
        upper_lower(AU,AL),
        chop_name(AL,A),
        check_duplicate_attrib_es(FILE1,A),
        display_attribs(FILE1),
        !,
        ask_attribs_es2(FILE1).

ask_attribs_es2(FILE1):-
        write("> Any more attributes (Y/N)? "),
        readln(ANS),
        upper_lower("Y",ANS),
        write(" Enter one attribute per line ..."),nl,
        write(" When done, press Return"),nl,
        !,
        ask_attribs_es2(FILE1).
```

```
ask_attribs_es2(FILE1):-
        check_null_file1(FILE1),
        !,
        explaingroup(FILE1),
        editkeys_es(FILE1).

ask_attribs_es2(_).

check_duplicate_attrib_es(AFILE,NAME):-
        attribute_es(AFILE,X),
        X=NAME,
        write("> Duplicate names not allowed"),nl,
        write("  Give some other name"),nl,
        !.

check_duplicate_attrib_es(AFILE,NAME):-
        attribute_ew(AFILE,_,Z),
        Z=NAME,
        write("> Duplicate names not allowed"),nl,
        write("  Give some other name"),nl,
        !.

check_duplicate_attrib_es(AFILE,ATTRIB):-
        assertz(attribute_es(AFILE,ATTRIB)).

check_null_file1(FILE1):-
        findall(X,attribute_es(FILE1,X),L2),
        findall(Y,attribute_ew(FILE1,_,Y),L1),
        union(L,L1,L2),
        shiftwindow(3),
        check_null_file2(FILE1,L).

check_null_file2(FILE1,[]):-
        write("> You should give at least one attribute"),
        nl,nl,
        write("> Do you want to give attributes (Y/N)? "),
        readln(ANS),
        upper_lower("Y",ANS),
        write("  Enter one attribute per line ..."),nl,
        write("  When done, press Return "),nl,
        !,
        ask_attribs_es2(FILE1),
        fail.

check_null_file2("",[]):-
        !,
        fail.

check_null_file2(FILE1,[]):-
        retract(entity_strong(FILE1)),
        display_files,
        !,
        fail.

check_null_file2(FILE1,_):-
        display_attribs(FILE1),
        shiftwindow(3).
```

```
ask_file_names1:-
        clearwindow,
        write("> Enter below names of your data files,"),nl,
        write("  one per line ..."),nl,
        write("  When done, press Return"),nl,
        ask_file_names2.

ask_file_names2:-
        write("> "),
        readln(NAMEU),
        not (NAMEU=""),
        upper_lower(NAMEU,NAMEL),
        chop_name(NAMEL,NAME),
        check_duplicate_file(NAME),
        !,
        ask_file_names2.

ask_file_names2:-
        write("> Any more files (Y/N)? "),
        readln(ANS),
        upper_lower("Y",ANS),
        clearwindow,
        write("> Enter below names of your data files,"),nl,
        write("  one per line ..."),nl,
        write("  When done, press Return"),nl,
        !,
        ask_file_names2.

ask_file_names2.

check_duplicate_file(FILE1):-
        entity_strong(X),
        X=FILE1,nl,
        write("> Duplicate names not allowed"),nl,
        nl,
        write("> Press any key to continue ... "),nl,
        readchar(_),
        !,
        fail.

check_duplicate_file(T):-
        nfiles(X),
        Y = X+1,
        not (Y>15),
        assertz(entity_strong(T)),
        display_files,
        retract(nfiles(_)),
        asserta(nfiles(Y)),
        !.

check_duplicate_file(_):-
        write("> Max. No of files(15)  exceeded"),nl,
        nl,
        write("> Press any key to continue ... "),
        readchar(_),
        !,
        fail.
```

```
editkeys_es(FILE):-
        key_es(_,_),
        !,
        clearwindow,
        write("> Now  for file: "),
        write(FILE),nl,
        field_attr(0,15,25,14),
        ask_keys1(FILE,"").

editkeys_es(_).
```

```
/**********************/
/*      EDITOR        */
/**********************/
```

```
/***************************************************************************/
/*                                                                         */
/*    PURPOSE:                    TO ALLOW THE USER TO CHANGE THE INPUTS    */
/*                                HE HAS MADE ONCE                          */
/*                                                                         */
/*    TOP LEVEL PREDICATE         next_step                                */
/*                                                                         */
/*    SCREEN NUMBERS              14                                       */
/*                                                                         */
/***************************************************************************/
```

```
/***************************/
/* SUB-SECTIONS OF EDITOR  */
/***************************/
```

```
/***************************************************************************/
/*                                                                         */
/*    PURPOSE:                    EDITING OF FILES                         */
/*                                                                         */
/*    TOP LEVEL PREDICATE         edit_files                              */
/*                                                                         */
/***************************************************************************/
```

PREDICATES

```
        edit_files
        edit_files1(integer)
        deletefile1(symbol)
        deletefile2(symbol)
        renamefile1
        renamefile2(symbol,symbol)
```

CLAUSES

```
edit_files:-
        clearwindow,
        write("> "),
        menu(16,40,"EDIT FILES",
                ["ADD A FILE",
                 "DELETE A FILE",
                 "RENAME A FILE",
                 "QUIT"],
        CHOICE),
        edit_files1(CHOICE).

edit_files1(O):-
        !.
```

```
edit_files1(1):-
        clearwindow,
        write("> Input file name to add "),nl,
        write("> "),
        readln(NAMEU),
        not (NAMEU=""),
        upper_lower(NAMEU,NAMEL),
        chop_name(NAMEL,NAME),
        check_duplicate_file(NAME),
        entity_strong(NAME),
        write(" Enter one attribute per line ..."),nl,
        write(" When done, press Return"),nl,
        ask_attribs_es2(NAME).

edit_files1(1).

edit_files1(2):-
        clearwindow,
        write("> Give the file name to delete"),nl,
        write("> "),
        readln(NAMEU),
        upper_lower(NAMEU,NAME),
        not (NAME=""),
        !,
        clearwindow,
        write("> Deleting File: "),
        write(NAME),nl,nl,
        write(">     ** CAUTION  **"),nl,nl,
        write("  On deleting the file all other related"),nl,
        write("   information (attributes, groups, keys)"),nl,
        write("   will also be lost"),nl,nl,
        write("> Proceed with delete (Y/N)?"),
        readln(ANS),
        upper_lower("Y",ANS),
        deletefile1(NAME).

edit_files1(2):-
        !.

edit_files1(3):-
        clearwindow,
        renamefile1.

edit_files1(_).

deletefile1(A):-
        retract(entity_strong(A)),
        !,
        deletefile2(A).

deletefile1(_):-
        write("> No such file"),nl,nl,
        write("> Press any key to continue ..."),
        readchar(_),
        !.
```

```
deletefile2(A):-
        retract(entity_weak(A,_)),
        fail.

deletefile2(A):-
        retract(attribute_es(A,_)),
        fail.

deletefile2(A):-
        retract(attribute_ew(A,_,_)),
        fail.

deletefile2(A):-
        retract(key_es([A],_)),
        fail.

deletefile2(_):-
        display_files.

renamefile1:-
        clearwindow,
        write("> Give the name of file to rename"),nl,
        write("> "),
        readln(NAMEU),
        upper_lower(NAMEU,NAME),
        entity_strong(NAME),
        !,
        write("> Give the new name"),nl,
        write("> "),
        readln(NAMEU1),
        upper_lower(NAMEU1,NAMEL1),
        chop_name(NAMEL1,NAME1),
        renamefile2(NAME,NAME1).

renamefile1:-
        write("> No such file exists"),nl,nl,
        write("> Press any key to continue ..."),
        readchar(_).

renamefile2(A,B):-
        retract(entity_strong(A)),
        asserta(entity_strong(B)),
        fail.

renamefile2(A,B):-
        retract(entity_weak(A,X)),
        asserta(entity_weak(B,X)),
        fail.

renamefile2(A,B):-
        retract(attribute_es(A,X)),
        asserta(attribute_es(B,X)),
        fail.

renamefile2(A,B):-
        retract(attribute_ew(A,X,Y)),
        asserta(attribute_ew(B,X,Y)),
        fail.
```

```
renamefile2(A,B):-
        retract(key_es([A],X)),
        asserta(key_es([B],X)),
        fail.

renamefile2(_,_):-
        display_files.
```

```
/**********************************************************************/
/*                                                                  */
/*    PURPOSE:                    EDITING OF ATTRIBUTES             */
/*                                                                  */
/*    TOP LEVEL PREDICATE         edit_attrib_menu                  */
/*                                                                  */
/**********************************************************************/


PREDICATES
        confirm
        edit_attrib1(symbol)
        edit_attrib_menu
        edit_attrib(integer)
        delete_attrib_file1(symbol,symbol)
        delete_attrib_file2(symbol,symbol)
        delete_attrib_file3(symbol,symbol)
        delete_attrib_file4(symbol,symbol)
        delete_attrib_file5(symbol)
        delete_attrib_group1(symbol,symbol)
        delete_attrib_group2(symbol,symbol,symbol)
        delete_attrib_group3(symbol,symbol,symbol)
        delete_attrib_group4(symbol,symbol,symbol)
        delete_attrib_group5(symbol,symbol)
        edit_attrib_group1(symbol,symbol)


CLAUSES


confirm:-
        write(">        ** CAUTION ** "),nl,nl,
        write("> All other relted information will"),
        write("  also be lost with delete"),nl,nl,
        write("> Proceed with delete Y/N? "),
        readln(ANS),
        upper_lower("Y",ANS),
        !.

confirm:-
        fail.

edit_attrib1(FILE1):-
        clearwindow,
        write("> Please give the file name whose"),nl,
        write("  attributes you want to edit"),nl,
        write("> "),
        readln(FILEU),
        upper_lower(FILEU,FILE1),
        entity_strong(FILE1),
        display_attribs(FILE1),
        !.

edit_attrib1(_):-
        write("> No such file"),nl,nl,
        write("> Press any key to continue ..."),
        readchar(_),
        fail.
```

```
edit_attrib_group1(FILE1,GROUP):-
        write("> Input the group name of interest"),nl,
        write("> "),
        readln(GROUPU),
        upper_lower(GROUPU,GROUP),
        entity_weak(FILE1,GROUP),
        !.

edit_attrib_group1(_,_):-
        write("> No such group"),nl,nl,
        write("> Press any key to continue ..."),
        readchar(_),
        fail.

delete_attrib_group1(FILE1,GROUP):-
        clearwindow,
        write("> Give the attribute to delete"),nl,
        write("> "),
        readln(NAMEU),
        upper_lower(NAMEU,NAME),
        attribute_ew(FILE1,GROUP,NAME),
        !,
        delete_attrib_group2(FILE1,GROUP,NAME).

delete_attrib_group1(_,_):-
        write("> No such attribute"),nl,nl,
        write("> Press any key to continue ..."),nl,
        readchar(_).

delete_attrib_group2(FILE1,GROUP,NAME):-
        clearwindow,
        write("> Deleting attribute: "),
        write(NAME),nl,nl,
        confirm,
        delete_attrib_group3(FILE1,GROUP,NAME),
        !.

delete_attrib_group2(_,_,_).

delete_attrib_group3(FILE1,GROUP,NAME):-
        retract(attribute_ew(FILE1,GROUP,NAME)),
        display_attribs(FILE1),
        findall(X,attribute_ew(FILE1,GROUP,X),L),
        check_null_group(FILE1,GROUP,L),
        entity_weak(FILE1,GROUP),
        delete_attrib_group4(FILE1,GROUP,NAME),
        !.

delete_attrib_group3(FILE1,GROUP,_):-
        display_attribs(FILE1),
        retract(key_ew([FILE1],[GROUP],_)),
        fail.

delete_attrib_group3(FILE1,_,_):-
        display_keys(FILE1),
        check_null_file1(FILE1),
        !.

delete_attrib_group3(_,_,_).
```

```
delete_attrib_group4(FILE1,GROUP,NAME):-
        key_ew([FILE1],[GROUP],X),
        member(NAME,X),
        retract(key_ew([FILE1],[GROUP],X)),
        delete_attrib_group5(FILE1,GROUP),
        fail.

delete_attrib_group4(_,_,_).

delete_attrib_group5(FILE1,GROUP):-
        display_keys(FILE1),
        key_ew([FILE1],[GROUP],_),
        !.

delete_attrib_group5(FILE1,GROUP):-
        write("> Group: "),
        write(GROUP),nl,nl,
        write("  Does not have any key after delete"),nl,nl,
        write("> It must have at least one key"),nl,
        ask_keys1(FILE1,GROUP).

delete_attrib_file1(FILE1,NAME):-
        attribute_es(FILE1,NAME),
        delete_attrib_file2(FILE1,NAME),
        !.

delete_attrib_file1(_,_):-
        write("> No such attribute"),nl,nl,
        write("> Press any key to continue ...."),
        readchar(_).

delete_attrib_file2(FILE1,NAME):-
        clearwindow,
        write("> Deleting attribute: "),
        write(NAME),nl,nl,
        confirm,
        retract(attribute_es(FILE1,NAME)),
        display_attribs(FILE1),
        !,
        check_null_file1(FILE1),
        delete_attrib_file3(FILE1,NAME).

delete_attrib_file2(_,_).

delete_attrib_file3(FILE1,NAME):-
        entity_strong(FILE1),
        !,
        delete_attrib_file4(FILE1,NAME).

delete_attrib_file3(FILE1,_):-
        deletefile2(FILE1).

delete_attrib_file4(FILE1,NAME):-
        key_es([FILE1],X),
        member(NAME,X),
        retract(key_es([FILE1],X)),
        delete_attrib_file5(FILE1),
        fail.

delete_attrib_file4(_,_).
```

```
delete_attrib_file5(FILE1):-
        display_keys(FILE1),
        key_es([FILE1],_),
        !.

delete_attrib_file5(FILE):-
        clearwindow,
        write("> File : "),
        write(FILE),nl,
        write("> Does not has any key after delete"),nl,nl,
        write("  It must have at least one key"),nl,
        ask_keys1(FILE,"").

edit_attrib_menu:-
        clearwindow,
        write("> "),
        menu(16,40,"EDIT ATTRIBUTES",
                ["ADD TO A GROUP",
                 "DELETE FROM A GROUP",
                 "ADD TO A FILE",
                 "DELETE FROM A FILE",
                 "QUIT"],
        CHOICE),
        edit_attrib(CHOICE).

edit_attrib(0):-
        !.

edit_attrib(1):-
        edit_attrib1(FILE1),
        edit_attrib_group1(FILE1,GROUP),
        ask_attrib_ew(FILE1,GROUP),
        !.

edit_attrib(1):-
        !.

edit_attrib(2):-
        edit_attrib1(FILE1),
        edit_attrib_group1(FILE1,GROUP),
        delete_attrib_group1(FILE1,GROUP),
        !.

edit_attrib(2):-
        !.

edit_attrib(3):-
        edit_attrib1(FILE1),
        clearwindow,
        write("> Input the attributes one by one"),nl,
        write("  At end press Return"),nl,
        ask_attribs_es2(FILE1),
        !.

edit_attrib(3):-
        !.
```

```
edit_attrib(4):-
        edit_attrib1(FILE1),
        clearwindow,
        write("> Please give the attribute to delete"),nl,
        write("> "),
        readln(NAMEU),
        upper_lower(NAMEU,NAME),
        delete_attrib_file1(FILE1,NAME),
        !.

edit_attrib(4):-
        !.
```

```
/*********************************************************************/
/*                                                                   */
/*    PURPOSE:                    EDITING OF GROUPS                   */
/*                                                                   */
/*    TOP LEVEL PREDICATE         edit_groups                        */
/*                                                                   */
/*********************************************************************/


PREDICATES

        edit_groups
        edit_groups1(integer,symbol)
        add_groups1(symbol)
        deletegroup1(symbol,symbol)
        deletegroup2(symbol,symbol)
        renamegroup1(symbol)
        renamegroup2(symbol,symbol,symbol)

CLAUSES

edit_groups:-
        clearwindow,
        write("> Input the file name of which "),nl,
        write("  you want to edit the groups "),nl,nl,
        write("> "),
        readln(NAMEU),
        upper_lower(NAMEU,NAME),
        entity_strong(NAME),
        !,
        display_attribs(NAME),
        clearwindow,
        write("> "),
        menu(16,40,"EDIT GROUPS",
                ["ADD A GROUP",
                 "DELETE A GROUP",
                 "RENAME A GROUP",
                 "QUIT"],
        CHOICE),
        edit_groups1(CHOICE,NAME).

edit_groups:-
        write("> No such file"),nl,nl,
        write("> Press any key to continue ..."),
        readchar(_),
        !.


edit_groups1(0,_):-
        !.

edit_groups1(1,FILE1):-
        add_groups1(FILE1),
        !.
```

```
edit_groups1(2,FILE1):-
        clearwindow,
        write("> Give the group name to delete"),nl,
        write("> "),
        readln(NAMEU),
        upper_lower(NAMEU,NAME),
        not (NAME=""),
        clearwindow,
        write("> Deleting Group: "),
        write(NAME),nl,nl,
        write(">     ** NOTE  **"),nl,nl,
        write("  On deleting the group, the attributes"),nl,
        write("  will not be deleted from the file"),nl,nl,
        write("> Proceed with delete (Y/N)?"),
        readln(ANS),
        upper_lower("Y",ANS),
        deletegroup1(NAME,FILE1),
        !.

edit_groups1(2,_):-
        !.

edit_groups1(3,FILE1):-
        clearwindow,
        renamegroup1(FILE1),
        !.

edit_groups1(_,_).


add_groups1(FILE1):-
        entity_strong(FILE1),
        !,
        ask_groups_es1(FILE1).

add_groups1(_):-
        write("> No such file"),nl,nl,
        write("> No such file exists"),nl,nl,
        write("> Press any key to continue ..."),
        readchar(_).

deletegroup1(NAME,FILE1):-
        retract(entity_weak(FILE1,NAME)),
        !,
        deletegroup2(NAME,FILE1).

deletegroup1(_,_):-
        write("> No such group"),nl,nl,
        write("> Press any key to continue ..."),
        readchar(_).

deletegroup2(NAME,FILE):-
        retract(attribute_ew(FILE,NAME,X)),
        asserta(attribute_es(FILE,X)),
        fail.

deletegroup2(_,FILE):-
        display_attribs(FILE).
```

```
renamegroup1(FILE1):-
        write("> Give the name of group to rename"),nl,
        write("> "),
        readln(NAMEU),
        upper_lower(NAMEU,NAME),
        entity_weak(FILE1,NAME),
        !,
        write("> Give the new name"),nl,
        write("> "),
        readln(NAMEU1),
        upper_lower(NAMEU1,NAMEL1),
        chop_name(NAMEL1,NAME1),
        renamegroup2(NAME,NAME1,FILE1).

renamegroup1(_):-
        write("> No such group"),nl,nl,
        write("> Press any key to continue ..."),
        readchar(_).

renamegroup2(A,B,FILE1):-
        retract(entity_weak(FILE1,A)),
        asserta(entity_weak(FILE1,B)),
        fail.

renamegroup2(A,B,FILE1):-
        retract(attribute_ew(FILE1,A,Y)),
        asserta(attribute_ew(FILE1,B,Y)),
        fail.

renamegroup2(_,_,FILE):-
        display_attribs(FILE).
```

```
/*************************************************************************/
/*                                                                     */
/*    PURPOSE:              MAIN MENU FOR EDITING                       */
/*                                                                     */
/*    TOP LEVEL PREDICATE   nextstep                                   */
/*                                                                     */
/*************************************************************************/


PREDICATES

        edit1
        edit2(integer)
        nextstep
        nextstep1(integer)

CLAUSES

edit1:-
        menu(16,40,"Editing of",
                ["FILES",
                 "GROUPS",
                 "ATTRIBUTES  ",
                 "QUIT  "],
                 CHOICE),
        edit2(CHOICE).


edit2(0):-
        !.

edit2(1):-
        edit_files,
        !.

edit2(2):-
        edit_groups,
        !.

edit2(3):-
        edit_attrib_menu,
        !.

edit2(_):-
        !.
```

```
nextstep:-
        clearwindow,
        write("> "),
        menu(16,40,"NEXT STEP",
                ["EDIT THE DATA",
                 "PROCEED WITH DIALOG"],
                CHOICE),
        nextstep1(CHOICE).

nextstep1(0):-
        !.

nextstep1(1):-
        edit1,
        !,
        nextstep.

nextstep1(_).
```

```
/************************************************************************/
/*                                                                    */
/*    PURPOSE:                OVERALL CONTROL OF THE INPUT OF          */
/*                            THE DIALOG THAT ACCEPTS THE USER         */
/*                            INPUTS OF THE DATA ITEMS                 */
/*                                                                    */
/*    TOP LEVEL PREDICATE     inputdata                               */
/*                                                                    */
/*    SCREEN NUMBERS          5-13                                    */
/*                                                                    */
/************************************************************************/


PREDICATES

        inputdata
        askes1
        askes2a

CLAUSES

inputdata:-
        write(">  Can you already foresee the data files you will need
        readln(ANS),                                    (Y/N) ?"
        upper_lower("Y",ANS),
        !,
        askes1,
        nextstep.

inputdata:-
        removewindow,removewindow,
        makewindow(3,2,11,"DIALOG",15,35,10,45),
        clearwindow,
        write("> Input the attributes you wish to store"),nl,
        write("  Give one attribute per line ..."),nl,
        write("  At end press Return"),nl,
        makewindow(5,52,7,"ATTRIBUTES",0,34,14,45),
        shiftwindow(3),
        ask_attribs_es2(""),
        entity_weak(_,_),
        !,
        askes2a,
        nextstep.

inputdata:-
        makewindow(4,0,0,"",7,1,3,3),
        asserta(entity_strong("flat file")),
        retract(attribute_es("",X)),
        asserta(attribute_es("flat file",X)),
        fail.

inputdata.
askes1:-
        removewindow,removewindow,
        makewindow(3,2,11,"DIALOG",15,35,10,45),
        makewindow(4,0,0,"",7,1,3,3),
        shiftwindow(3),
        ask_file_names1,
        fail.
```

```
askes1:-
        entity_strong(_),           /* Checks existence of files */
        !,
        ask_attribs_es1.
askes2a:-
        makewindow(4,0,0,"",7,1,3,3),
        shiftwindow(3),
        clearwindow,
        write("> To begin with we will make one file"),nl,
        write("  for each group."),nl,nl,
        write("  Attributes which are not in any group"),nl,
        write("  will be put in a file named 'ungrouped'."),nl,nl ,
        write("> Press any key to continue...."),
        readchar(_),
        fail.

askes2a:-
        retract(entity_weak("",X)),
        asserta(entity_strong(X)),
        fail.

askes2a:-
        retract(attribute_ew("",X,A)),
        asserta(attribute_es(X,A)),
        fail.

askes2a:-
        findall(X,attribute_es("",X),L),
        not(equal(L,[])),
        asserta(entity_strong(ungrouped)),
        retract(attribute_es("",X)),
        asserta(attribute_es(ungrouped,X)),
        fail.

askes2a:-
        display_files,
        fail.

askes2a:-
        clearwindow,
        write("> In these files, you might be able"),nl,
        write("  to further group the attributes."),nl,nl,
        write("> Press any key to continue ...."),
        readchar(_),
        entity_strong(X),
        display_files,
        clearwindow,
        ask_groups_es(X),
        fail.

askes2a.
```

```
/*********************************************************************/
/*                                                                 */
/*               FILE        :    FDS.PRO                           */
/*                                                                 */
/*               The predicates in  this  file conduct the dialog  to  */
/*               infer the fuctional dependencies                  */
/*                                                                 */
/*********************************************************************/
```

```
/*********************************************************************/
/*                                                                 */
/*    PURPOSE:                TO INFER THE FD'S BASED ON KEY        */
/*                                                                 */
/*    TOP LEVEL PREDICATE     keys                                 */
/*                                                                 */
/*    SCREEN NUMBERS          15-18                                */
/*                                                                 */
/*********************************************************************/
```

PREDICATES

```
        keys
        explain_key
        ask_keys
        ask_keys_es(symbol)
        ask_keys_ew(symbol)
        ask_keys1(symbol,symbol)
        ask_keys2(symbol,symbol)
        ask_keys3(symbol,symbol,list,list)
        check_key(symbol,symbol,list)
        check_existence(symbol,symbol,symbol,list,list)
```

CLAUSES

```
keys:-
        explain_key,
        ask_keys.
```

```
/****************************************************/
/*                                                  */
/*        FILE:    KEY_DEF.TXT                       */
/*                                                  */
/*   >  In every file/group there will be an        */
/*      identifier : an attribute or a group        */
/*      of attributes called the:                   */
/*                  KEY                              */
/*      whose vlaue is unique  for  all  the        */
/*      entries in that file or group               */
/*      (see example).                              */
/*                                                  */
/*      Press any key to continue ...               */
/*                                                  */
/****************************************************/
/*                                                  */
/*        FILE:    KEY_EG.TXT                        */
/*                                                  */
/*   For a STUDENTS file:                           */
/*                                                  */
/*   ROLL NO      NAME        CLASS                  */
/*   8769         Kasturi     M.Tech.               */
/*   8734         Vijay       B.Tech.               */
/*                                                  */
/*   ROLL NO is unique for all the                  */
/*   entries in this file.                          */
/*                                                  */
/*   Hence ROLL NO is a KEY.                        */
/*                                                  */
/****************************************************/

explain_key:-
        shiftwindow(3),
        clearwindow,
        file_str("keys_def.txt",C),
        write(C),
        field_attr(3,15,3,79),
        field_attr(4,17,7,15),
        makewindow(9,26,7,"EXAMPLE OF KEY",8,0,16,35),
        file_str("keys_eg.txt",B),
        write(B),
        field_attr(3,1,7,79),
        field_attr(5,1,4,31),
        field_attr(6,1,4,31),
        readchar(_),
        removewindow,
        shiftwindow(3),
        fail.

explain_key:-
        makewindow(6,90,10,"KEY",4,1,4,31),
        write("attribute(s) that determine"),nl,
        write("values of all attributes "),
        shiftwindow(3),
        fail.
```

```
explain_key:-
        clearwindow,
        write("> In general, there may be more than"),nl,
        write("  one key in a file (or a group)."),nl,
        nl,nl,
        write("> Press any key to continue ...."),nl,
        readchar(_),
        fail.

explain_key:-
        !.

ask_keys:-
        makewindow(7,32,7,"KEYS",8,14,17,20),
        shiftwindow(3),
        fail.

ask_keys:-
        entity_strong(FILE1),
        display_files,
        shiftwindow(3),
        display_attribs(FILE1),
        shiftwindow(3),
        ask_keys_es(FILE1),
        fail.

ask_keys.

ask_keys1(FILE1,GROUP):-
        ask_keys2(FILE1,GROUP),
        write("> Are there any more keys (Y/N) ?"),
        readln(ANS1),
        upper_lower("Y",ANS1),
        !,
        ask_keys1(FILE1,GROUP).

ask_keys1(FILE1,""):-
        key_es([FILE1],_),
        !.

ask_keys1(FILE1,""):-
        nl,
        write("> There must be at least one key "),nl,
        !,
        ask_keys1(FILE1,"").

ask_keys1(FILE1,X):-
        key_ew([FILE1],[X],_),
        !.


ask_keys1(FILE1,GROUP):-
        nl,
        write("> There must be at least one key "),nl,
        !,
        ask_keys1(FILE1,GROUP).
```

```
ask_keys2(FILE1,GROUP):-
        write("> Enter the attributes that form a key,"),nl,
        write("  Enter one attribute per line,"),nl,
        write("  When done, press return"),nl,
        ask_keys3(FILE1,GROUP,KEY1,[]),
        check_key(FILE1,GROUP,KEY1),
        display_keys(FILE1),
        !,
        write("> Are there any more keys (Y/N) ?"),
        readln(ANS1),
        upper_lower("Y",ANS1),
        ask_keys2(FILE1,GROUP).

ask_keys2(_,_).

ask_keys3(FILE1,GROUP,KEY1,IN):-
        write("> "),
        readln(NAMEU),
        not (NAMEU=""),
        upper_lower(NAMEU,NAME),
        !,
        check_existence(FILE1,GROUP,NAME,IN,OUT),
        ask_keys3(FILE1,GROUP,KEY1,OUT).

ask_keys3(FILE1,GROUP,KEY1,IN):-
        write("> Any more attributes in the key (Y/N)?"),
        readln(ANS),
        upper_lower("Y",ANS),
        !,
        ask_keys3(FILE1,GROUP,KEY1,IN).

ask_keys3(_,_,KEY1,KEY1).


check_existence(FILE1,"",NAME,IN,OUT):-
        attribute_es(FILE1,X),
        X=NAME,
        !,
        union(OUT,[NAME],IN).

check_existence(FILE1,"",NAME,IN,OUT):-
        attribute_ew(FILE1,_,X),
        X=NAME,
        !,
        union(OUT,[NAME],IN).

check_existence(FILE1,GROUP,NAME,IN,OUT):-
        attribute_ew(FILE1,GROUP,X),
        X=NAME,
        !,
        union(OUT,[NAME],IN).

check_existence(_,_,_,X,X):-
        write("> Undeclared/Mis-spelt attribute"),nl,
        !.
```

```
check_key(FILE1,"",KEY):-
        key_es([FILE1],X),
        equal(X,KEY),
        write("> This key is already known"),nl,
        !.

check_key(FILE1,GROUP,KEY):-
        key_ew([FILE1],[GROUP],X),
        equal(X,KEY),
        write("> This key is already known"),nl,
        !.

check_key(_,_,[]):-
        write("> Key must have at least one attribute"),nl,
        !.

check_key(FILE1,"",KEY1):-
        assertz(key_es([FILE1],KEY1)),
        !.

check_key(FILE1,GROUP,KEY1):-
        assertz(key_ew([FILE1],[GROUP],KEY1)).

ask_keys_es(FILE1):-
        clearwindow,
        ask_keys_ew(FILE1),
        write("> Now  for file: "),
        write(FILE1),nl,
        field_attr(0,15,25,11),
        display_attribs_ew(FILE1,""),
        ask_keys1(FILE1,"").

ask_keys_ew(FILE1):-
        entity_weak(FILE1,X),
        write("> For  group :  "),
        write(X),nl,
        field_attr(0,15,25,14),
        write("> In    file :  "),
        cursor(PP,_),
        write(FILE1),
        field_attr(PP,15,25,11),nl,
        display_attribs_ew(FILE1,X),
        ask_keys1(FILE1,X),
        clearwindow,
        fail.

ask_keys_ew(_).
```

```
/*****************************************************************************/
/*                                                                         */
/*      PURPOSE:                 TO INFER THE FD'S BASED ON  A             */
/*                               PART OF THE KEY                           */
/*                                                                         */
/*      TOP LEVEL PREDICATE      partfd                                    */
/*                                                                         */
/*      SCREEN NUMBERS           23-26                                     */
/*                                                                         */
/*****************************************************************************/
```

PREDICATES

```
        explain_partialfd
        partialfd
        getkey(symbol,symbol,list)
        partialfd1(symbol,symbol,list)
        partialfd2(symbol,symbol,list)
        read_part_key(list,list,list)
        read_part_attrib(symbol,symbol,symbol)
        checkname_pk_es(list,symbol,list,list)
```

CLAUSES

```
getkey(FILE,"",KEY):-
        entity_strong(FILE),
        key_es([FILE],KEY).

getkey(FILE,GROUP,KEY):-
        entity_weak(FILE,GROUP),
        key_ew([FILE],[GROUP],KEY).
```

```
/****************************************************/
/*                                                  */
/*       FILE:    PARTFD.TXT                         */
/*                                                  */
/*   Roll No    Name  Course  Grade                 */
/*                                                  */
/*    1267      ATUL  CADS     A                    */
/*    1267      ATUL  DPS      B                    */
/*    1267      ATUL  OR       C                    */
/*    1270      JOY   CADS     C                    */
/*    1270      JOY   DPS      B                    */
/*                                                  */
/*                                                  */
/*    Key  is  (Roll No, Course)                    */
/*    Name depends on only a part                   */
/*    of the key, i.e.  Roll No.                    */
/*                                                  */
/****************************************************/


explain_partialfd:-
        clearwindow,
        write("> Here we want to see if there are"),nl,
        write("  some attributes which depend on "),nl,
        write("  only a part of the key (see example)."),nl,nl,
        write("> Press any key to continue ..."),
        display_files,
        makewindow(2,26,7,"Example of part key",8,0,16,35),
        nl,
        file_str("partfd.txt",A),
        write(A),
        shiftwindow(3),
        readchar(_),
        makewindow(7,90,14,"KEYS",0,13,7,20),
        partialfd,
        !.

partialfd:-
        getkey(FILE1,GROUP,[X!XT]),
        not (equal (XT,[])),
        display_attribs_ew(FILE1,GROUP),
        shiftwindow(7),
        clearwindow,
        write("For Key :"),nl,
        writelist_hz([X!XT]),
        partialfd1(FILE1,GROUP,[X!XT]),
        fail.

partialfd.
```

```
partialfd1(_,_,_):-
        shiftwindow(3),
        clearwindow,
        fail.

partialfd1(FILE1,GROUP,KEY):-
        clearwindow,
        write("> For the Key shown in KEYS window:"),nl,nl,
        display_attribs(FILE1),
        write(" Is there any attribute which is affected"),nl,
        write(" by only a part of the key (Y/N)?"),
        readln(ANS),
        upper_lower("Y",ANS),
        partialfd2(FILE1,GROUP,KEY).

partialfd1(_,_,_).

partialfd2(FILE1,GROUP,KEY):-
        write("> Please enter the part key attributes"),nl,
        write("  one by one. When done, press Return"),nl,
        read_part_key(KEY,[],KEY1),
        read_part_attrib(FILE1,GROUP,NAME),
        asserta(fd(KEY1,[NAME])),
        write("> Any more such attributes (Y/N)?"),
        readln(A),
        upper_lower("Y",A),
        !,
        partialfd2(FILE1,GROUP,KEY).

partialfd2(_,_,_).

read_part_attrib(FILE1,"",NAME):-
        write("> Please type the affected attribute"),nl,
        write("> "),
        readln(NAMEU),
        upper_lower(NAMEU,NAME),
        attribute_es(FILE1,NAME),
        !.

read_part_attrib(FILE1,"",NAME):-
        write("> No such attribute"),nl,nl,
        write("> Do you want to give affected "),nl,
        write("  attribute   (Y/N)? "),
        readln(A),
        upper_lower("Y",A),
        !,
        read_part_attrib(FILE1,"",NAME).

read_part_attrib(_,"",_):-
        !,
        fail.

read_part_attrib(FILE1,GROUP,NAME):-
        write("> Please input the affected attribute"),nl,
        write("> "),
        readln(NAMEU),
        upper_lower(NAMEU,NAME),
        attribute_ew(FILE1,GROUP,NAME),
        !.
```

```
read_part_attrib(FILE1,GROUP,NAME):-
        write("> No such attribute"),nl,
        write("> Do you want to give affected ?"),nl,
        write("  attribute   (Y/N)? "),
        readln(A),
        upper_lower("Y",A),
        !,
        read_part_attrib(FILE1,GROUP,NAME).

read_part_attrib(_,_,_):-
        fail.

read_part_key(KEY,A,KEY1):-
        write("> "),
        readln(NAMEU),
        upper_lower(NAMEU,NAME),
        not (NAME=""),
        checkname_pk_es(KEY,NAME,A,X),
        !,
        read_part_key(KEY,X,KEY1).

read_part_key(KEY,A,KEY1):-
        write("> Any more attributes in part key (Y/N)?"),
        readln(ANS),
        upper_lower("Y",ANS),
        !,
        read_part_key(KEY,A,KEY1).

read_part_key(KEY,[],KEY1):-
        write("> You should give at least one attribute."),nl,nl,
        write("> Do you want to give the part key (Y/N)?"),
        readln(ANS),
        upper_lower("Y",ANS),
        !,
        read_part_key(KEY,[],KEY1).

read_part_key(_,[],_):-
        !,
        fail.


read_part_key(_,A,A).


checkname_pk_es(KEY,NAME,A,X):-
        member(NAME,KEY),
        union (X,[NAME],A),
        !.

checkname_pk_es(_,_,A,A):-
        write("> It is not a member of this key"),nl,
        !,
        nl,
        write("> Input again"),nl.
```

```
/****************************************************************************/
/*                                                                        */
/*      PURPOSE:                      TO INFER THE FD'S IN WHICH A NON-KEY  */
/*                                    ATTRIBUTE DETERMINES A  KEY ATTRIBUTE */
/*                                                                        */
/*      TOP LEVEL PREDICATE           nonkeyfd                             */
/*                                                                        */
/*      SCREEN NUMBERS                19-20                                */
/*                                                                        */
/****************************************************************************/


PREDICATES

        nonkeyfd
        findall_key(list,symbol,symbol,list)
        readnonkey(list,list,list)
        readnonkey1(list,list,list,symbol)
        nonkeyfd4(list,list)
        nonkeyfd3(list,symbol)
        nonkeyfd2(list,list)
        nonkeyfd1(symbol,symbol)

CLAUSES

nonkeyfd:-
        makewindow(7,90,14,"KEY ATTRIBUTES",0,13,7,20),
        shiftwindow(5),
        removewindow,
        makewindow(5,52,7,"NON KEY ATTRIBUTES",0,34,14,46),
        shiftwindow(3),
        clearwindow,
        write("> Locate the window titled KEY ATTRIBUTES"),nl,
        field_attr(0,26,15,14),
        write("  on the screen (upper left corner) and"),nl,
        write("  Also the NON KEY ATTRIBUTES window (up)"),nl,
        write("  Proceed now keeping  these two windows"),nl,
        write("  in mind."),nl,nl,
        write("> Press any key to continue ...."),
        readchar(_),
        fail.

nonkeyfd:-
        clearwindow,
        write("> Normally key attributes will determine"),nl,
        write("  the values of non-key attributes."),nl,nl,
        write("  However, there may be exceptions."),nl,nl,
        write("> Press any key to continue ...."),
        readchar(_),
        fail.

nonkeyfd:-
        entity_strong(FILE1),
        shiftwindow(3),
        clearwindow,
        nonkeyfd1(FILE1,""),
        fail.
```

```
nonkeyfd:-
        entity_weak(FILE1,GROUP),
        shiftwindow(3),
        clearwindow,
        nonkeyfd1(FILE1,GROUP),
        fail.

nonkeyfd:-
        shiftwindow(7),
        removewindow,
        shiftwindow(5),
        clearwindow,
        shiftwindow(3).

nonkeyfd1(FILE1,GROUP):-
        findall_att(FILE1,GROUP,ALL),
        findall_key([],FILE1,GROUP,ALLKEY),
        minus(NONKEY,ALL,ALLKEY),
        not(equal(NONKEY,[])),
        !,
        shiftwindow(7),
        clearwindow,
        writelist_hz(ALLKEY),
        shiftwindow(5),
        clearwindow,
        cursor(T,R),
        disp_list_col(T,R,NONKEY),
        shiftwindow(3),
        write("> In above windows do you see any key"),nl,
        write("  attribute whose  value  depends  on "),nl,
        write("  some of the non-key attributes (Y/N)?  "),
        readln(ANS),
        upper_lower("Y",ANS),
        nonkeyfd2(ALLKEY,NONKEY),
        fail.

nonkeyfd1(_,_).


findall_key(A,FILE1,"",ALLKEY):-
        key_es([FILE1],L),
        union(M,L,A),
        not (equal (M,A)),
        !,
        findall_key(M,FILE1,"",ALLKEY).

findall_key(A,_,"",A).

nonkeyfd2(KEY,NONKEY):-
        nonkeyfd4(NONKEY,Q),
        nonkeyfd3(KEY,P),
        asserta(fd(Q,[P])).

nonkeyfd2(KEY,NONKEY):-
        clearwindow,
        write("> Any more Key attribute whose value"),nl,
        write("  depends on Non-key attributes (Y/N)? "),
        readln(ANS),
        upper_lower("Y",ANS),
        !,
        nonkeyfd2(KEY,NONKEY).
```

```prolog
nonkeyfd2(_,_).

nonkeyfd3(KEY,P):-
        write("> Input the  key attribute."),nl,
        write("> "),
        readln(NAMEU),
        upper_lower(NAMEU,NAME),
        member(NAME,KEY),
        P=NAME,
        !.

nonkeyfd3(KEY,P):-
        write("> This attribute is not in key"),nl,nl,
        write("> Do you want to input again (Y/N)?"),
        readln(ANS),
        upper_lower("Y",ANS),
        !,
        nonkeyfd3(KEY,P).

nonkeyfd3(_,_):-
        !,
        fail.

nonkeyfd4(NONKEY,Q):-
        write("> Input such non key attributes one by one"),nl,
        write("  When done press return."),nl,
        readnonkey([],NONKEY,Q).

readnonkey(IN,NONKEY,OUT):-
        write("> "),
        readln(NAMEU),
        upper_lower(NAMEU,NAME),
        not(NAME=""),
        readnonkey1(IN,NONKEY,OUT1,NAME),
        !,
        readnonkey(OUT1,NONKEY,OUT).

readnonkey(A,NONKEY,B):-
        write("> Any more attributes (Y/N) ?"),
        readln(ANS),
        upper_lower("Y",ANS),
        !,
        readnonkey(A,NONKEY,B).

readnonkey([],NONKEY,B):-
        write("> You should give at least one"),nl,
        write("  attribute "),nl,nl,
        write("> Do you want to give (Y/N)?"),
        readln(ANS),
        upper_lower("Y",ANS),
        !,
        readnonkey([],NONKEY,B).

readnonkey([],_,_):-
        !,
        fail.

readnonkey(IN,_,IN).
```

```
readnonkey1(IN,NONKEY,OUT,NAME):-
        member(NAME,NONKEY),
        union(OUT,IN,[NAME]),
        !.

readnonkey1(IN,_,IN,_):-
        write("> It is not a non key attribute"),nl,
        write("> Input again"),nl.
```

```
/**************************************************************************/
/*                                                                      */
/*    PURPOSE:                    TO INFER MULTI VALUED DEPENDENCIES     */
/*                                                                      */
/*    TOP LEVEL PREDICATE         mvds                                  */
/*                                                                      */
/*    SCREEN NUMBERS              21-22                                 */
/*                                                                      */
/**************************************************************************/
```

PREDICATES

```
        mvds
        explainmvd
        mvd1
        mvd2(symbol)
        mvd3(symbol,symbol)
        mvd4(symbol,symbol,list)
        ask_md_attr(symbol,symbol,list)
        ask_md_attr1(symbol,symbol,symbol,list)
        ask_md_attr2(symbol,symbol,symbol,list,list)
        check_md_attr(symbol,symbol,symbol)
```

CLAUSES

```
/**************************************************/
/*                                              */
/*      FILE:    MVD_EG.TXT                      */
/*                                              */
/*   EXAMPLE :                                   */
/*                                              */
/*   ROLL NO    COURSES TAKEN                    */
/*   8765    IME602,CS601,IME624                 */
/*   8766    IME602,IME624,ME651                 */
/*   8767    IME602,IME673,IME621                */
/*   8769    HSS730,EE450                        */
/*                                              */
/*                                              */
/*   Here, COURSE TAKEN  can be seen            */
/*   to take several values for  any            */
/*   given value of the key, ROLL NO.           */
/*                                              */
/**************************************************/
```

```
explainmvd:-
        clearwindow,
        write("> Now we need to know which among the "),nl,
        write("  attributes listed can take several"),nl,
        write("  values  for any given value of the key"),nl,
        write("  (see example)."),nl,nl,
        makewindow(2,26,7,"'Multi valued attributes'",8,0,16,35),
        file_str("mvd_eg.txt",B),
        write(B),
        shiftwindow(3),
        write("> Press any key to continue ...."),
        readchar(_).
```

```
check_md_attr(_,_,""):-
        !,
        fail.

check_md_attr(FILE1,"",NAME):-
        key_es([FILE1],X),
        member(NAME,X),
        !,
        write("> This attribute is already in key."),nl,
        fail.

check_md_attr(FILE1,"",NAME):-
        retract(attribute_es(FILE1,NAME)),
        !.

check_md_attr(_,"",_):-
        !,
        write("> Undeclared/Misspelt attribute"),nl,
        fail.

check_md_attr(FILE1,GROUP,NAME):-
        key_ew([FILE1],[GROUP],X),
        member(NAME,X),
        !,
        write("> This attribute is already in key."),nl,
        fail.

check_md_attr(FILE1,GROUP,NAME):-
        retract(attribute_ew(FILE1,GROUP,NAME)),
        !.

check_md_attr(_,_,_):-
        write("> Undeclared/Misspelt attribute"),nl,
        fail.

ask_md_attr2(FILE1,GROUP,MD,IN,OUT):-
        write("> "),
        readln(NAMEU),
        upper_lower(NAMEU,NAME),
        check_md_attr(FILE1,GROUP,NAME),
        !,
        union(OUT1,IN,[NAME]),
        ask_md_attr2(FILE1,GROUP,MD,OUT1,OUT).

ask_md_attr2(FILE1,GROUP,NAME,IN,OUT):-
        write("> Any more attributes whose value"),nl,
        write("  depends on the value of : "),
        cursor(P,Q),
        write(NAME),
        field_attr(P,Q,14,12),nl,
        write("  (Y/N)? "),
        readln(ANS),
        upper_lower("Y",ANS),nl,
        !,
        write("> Enter the attributes one per line."),nl,
        write("> When done, Press return."),nl,
        ask_md_attr2(FILE1,GROUP,NAME,IN,OUT).

ask_md_attr2(_,_,_,X,X).
```

```
ask_md_attr1(FILE1,GROUP,NAME,RHS):-
        clearwindow,
        write("> Are there any attributes whose value"),nl,
        write("  depends on the value of : "),
        cursor(P,Q),
        write(NAME),nl,
        field_attr(P,Q,14,12),
        write("  (Y/N)? "),
        readln(ANS),
        upper_lower("Y",ANS),
        !,
        write("> Input such attributes one per line."),nl,
        write("  When done, press return."),nl,
        ask_md_attr2(FILE1,GROUP,NAME,[NAME],RHS).

ask_md_attr1(_,_,NAME,[NAME]).

ask_md_attr(FILE1,GROUP,KEY):-
        write("> "),
        readln(NAMEU),
        upper_lower(NAMEU,NAME),
        check_md_attr(FILE1,GROUP,NAME),
        ask_md_attr1(FILE1,GROUP,NAME,RHS),
        asserta(mvd(KEY,RHS)),
        fail.

ask_md_attr(FILE1,GROUP,KEY):-
        write("> Any  more attributes which can   take "),nl,
        write("  more than one value for same value of"),nl,
        write("  the key (Y/N)? "),
        readln(ANS),
        upper_lower(ANS,"Y"),
        !,
        write("> Enter the attribute"),nl,
        ask_md_attr(FILE1,GROUP,KEY).

mvd2(FILE1):-
        entity_weak(FILE1,GROUP),
        mvd3(FILE1,GROUP),
        fail.

mvd2(_).

mvd4(_,_,_):-
        shiftwindow(3),
        clearwindow,
        fail.

mvd4(_,_,X):-
        shiftwindow(7),
        clearwindow,
        writelist_hz(X),
        fail.
```

```
mvd4(FILE1,GROUP,X):-
        shiftwindow(3),
        write("> Is there any attribute above which can"),nl,
        write("  take several values for a single value"),nl,
        write("  of the key  (Y/N)? "),
        readln(ANS),
        upper_lower(ANS,"Y"),
        clearwindow,
        write("> Enter the attribute"),nl,
        ask_md_attr(FILE1,GROUP,X).


mvd3(FILE1,GROUP):-
        getkey(FILE1,GROUP,X),
        findall_att(FILE1,GROUP,ALL),
        findall_key([],FILE1,GROUP,ALLKEY),
        minus(NONKEY,ALL,ALLKEY),
        not(equal(NONKEY,[])),
        shiftwindow(5),
        clearwindow,
        cursor(T,R),
        disp_list_col(T,R,NONKEY),
        shiftwindow(3),
        mvd4(FILE1,GROUP,X),
        fail.

mvd3(_,_).

mvd1:-
        entity_strong(FILE1),
        mvd2(FILE1),
        mvd3(FILE1,""),
        fail.

mvd1.

mvds:-
        explainmvd,
        makewindow(7,90,7,"Keys",0,13,7,20),
        mvd1,
        shiftwindow(2),
        removewindow,
        shiftwindow(3).
```

```
/***********************************************************************/
/*                                                                     */
/*    PURPOSE:                  MAIN CONTROL FOR INFERENCE OF FD'S      */
/*                                                                     */
/*    TOP LEVEL PREDICATE       fds                                    */
/*                                                                     */
/***********************************************************************/
```

PREDICATES

```
        fds
        assertfds
```

CLAUSES

```
fds:-
        shiftwindow(2),
        removewindow,
        shiftwindow(6),
        removewindow,
        shiftwindow(7),
        removewindow,
        shiftwindow(3),
        fail.

fds:-
        nonkeyfd,
        mvds,
        fail.

fds:-
        getkey(_,_,[_|XT]),
        not (equal (XT,[])),
        !,
        explain_partialfd,
        shiftwindow(2),
        removewindow,
        shiftwindow(7),
        removewindow,
        shiftwindow(3),
        assertfds.

fds:-
        assertfds.

assertfds:-
        key_es([FILE],X),
        attribute_es(FILE,Y),
        asserta(fd(X,[Y])),
        fail.

assertfds:-
        key_ew([FILE],[GROUP],X),
        attribute_ew(FILE,GROUP,Y),
        asserta(fd(X,[Y])),
        fail.
```

```
assertfds:-
        key_es([FILE],X),
        key_ew([FILE],_,Y),
        member(M,Y),
        asserta(fd(X,[M])),
        fail.

assertfds.
```

Lecture Notes in Computer Science